THE VEGETARIAN ON A DIET

A guide to an exciting range of vegetarian cooking which is of particular value to diabetics and those watching their weight.

THE VEGETARIAN ON A DIET

by

Margaret Cousins and Jill Metcalfe

Illustrated by Ian Jones

THORSONS PUBLISHERS LIMITED
Wellingborough, Northamptonshire

First published February 1984
Second Impression March 1984
Third Impression June 1984
Fourth Impression November 1984
Fifth Impression July 1985
Sixth Impression November 1985

British Library Cataloguing in Publication Data

Cousins, Margaret
   The vegetarian on a diet.
   1. Reducing diets — Recipes
   2. Vegetarian cookery
   I. Title   II. Metcalfe, Jill
   641.5'636   RM222.2

ISBN 0-7225-0887-5

Printed and bound in Great Britain

Contents

Why This Book?

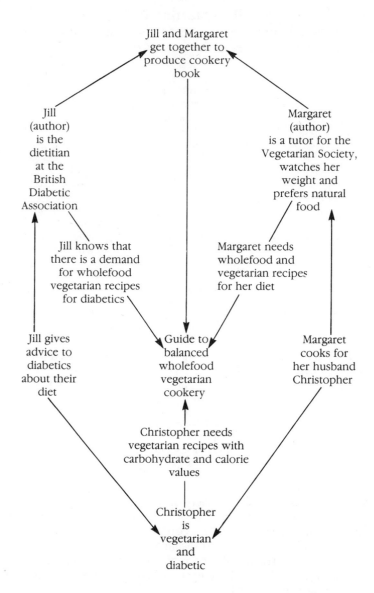

Jill and Margaret get together to produce cookery book

Jill (author) is the dietitian at the British Diabetic Association

Margaret (author) is a tutor for the Vegetarian Society, watches her weight and prefers natural food

Jill knows that there is a demand for wholefood vegetarian recipes for diabetics

Margaret needs wholefood and vegetarian recipes for her diet

Jill gives advice to diabetics about their diet

Guide to balanced wholefood vegetarian cookery

Margaret cooks for her husband Christopher

Christopher needs vegetarian recipes with carbohydrate and calorie values

Christopher is vegetarian and diabetic

Current research is indicating the benefits of a wholefood diet generally and specifically for diabetes (see Diabetic's Guide page 20). This is an approach to a natural meatless diet where both carbohydrates and calories are taken into account. It is therefore suitable for either the diabetic (whether insulin dependent or insulin independent), the weight-watcher or both.

Merely a Starting Point:

This book hopefully suggests some important directions and it is up to you to develop the idea further.

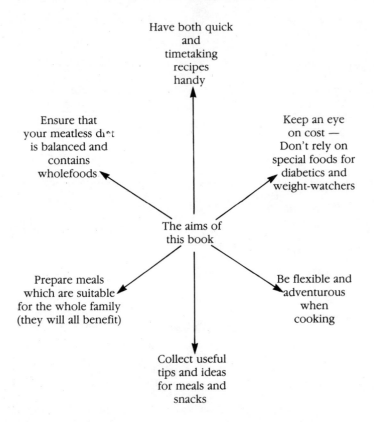

Have both quick
and
timetaking
recipes
handy

Ensure that
your meatless diet
is balanced and
contains
wholefoods

Keep an eye
on cost —
Don't rely on
special foods for
diabetics and
weight-watchers

The aims of
this book

Prepare meals
which are suitable
for the whole family
(they will all benefit)

Be flexible and
adventurous
when
cooking

Collect useful
tips and ideas
for meals and
snacks

People are vegetarian for a variety of reasons. They may be against the killing of animals: it may be to benefit their health; they may feel that the vegetarian diet is a more economical way of providing food for the world or they may just dislike meat.

Whatever their reasons, there is increasing evidence that a reduced meat diet may well be the best one for health generally and in certain cases can greatly improve it.

Vegetarian dishes, even when for special diets, can be exciting and good to eat — which is the reason for this book.

Introduction

The first part of this book is to introduce you to our approach to a wholefood meatless diet. This is followed by a section on making the most of vegetables and fruit and indicates the endless ways in which they can be used to form the main part of the meal.

Finally there are the recipe sections. Each part has its own foreword with the recipes listed where possible, in ascending order of their carbohydrate content. The main meals have been divided into two groups — one for when time for preparing food is limited, the other for when more time is available.

Thinking About Alternatives

The typical western diet, which relies heavily on processed carbohydrate, as well as animal fat and protein, often provides more calories than is necessary for most of us. It may well be less beneficial to our health in the long term than a more balanced, unrefined vegetarian diet.

So we are asking you to try a different, healthier way of eating by:

— making several substitutes for certain foods which until now you have probably automatically eaten in varying amounts.
— keeping an eye on the overall amount of calories you are taking in (although you may be doing this already).

We are assuming that you are familiar with the necessary background information regarding any medical condition which you may have. If any problems are encountered on this diet do not hesitate to consult your doctor or dietitian.

Balancing the Diet

A balanced diet should contain protein, carbohydrate, fat, vitamins, minerals and fibre. A wide variety of fruit and vegetables (including peas, beans, lentils and whole grains) can provide us with all of these.

Food — the different types and their energy (calorie) value

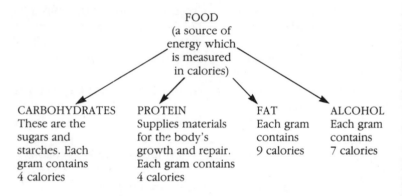

FOOD
(a source of energy which is measured in calories)

CARBOHYDRATES
These are the sugars and starches. Each gram contains 4 calories

PROTEIN
Supplies materials for the body's growth and repair. Each gram contains 4 calories

FAT
Each gram contains 9 calories

ALCOHOL
Each gram contains 7 calories

Any foods can provide excess calories in your diet. Fatty foods in particular are a problem as fats contain over twice as many calories as either carbohydrate or protein and the calories in alcohol are often forgotten about.

Vitamins and Minerals

Vitamins and minerals are important in the regulation of the body's processes. Vitamins also help in the body's resistance to disease, and minerals are important constituents of the body's structure, e.g. calcium in teeth and bones.

To Eat . . .

List A — Foods to Include in Your Diet

Whole grains (wheat, rice, oats etc., their flours and other
    products)
Fruit and vegetables
Pulses (peas, beans, lentils, peanuts)
Nuts and seeds (in moderation, since they are high in calories
    due to their fat content)

these provide

Protein (incomplete)
Provides energy (calories),
vitamins, minerals and some
of the ingredients necessary
for the building and repair
of our body proteins *but*
each of these need to be
taken with one of the
complete proteins (list B) or
with another incomplete
protein.* (See over.)

Carbohydrate (unprocessed)
Provides energy (calories),
fibre, vitamins and minerals.
Helps digestion, the fibre
providing bulk. Digestion
takes longer and this may
reduce blood sugar rises
(particularly important for
the diabetic).

List B — Foods to Include in Your Diet

Milk (low fat, skimmed)
Yogurt (low fat)
Cheese (low fat cottage, curd or quark cheese or medium fat
  hard cheese)
Eggs (in moderation)

these provide

Protein (complete)
Provides energy (calories),
vitamins and minerals and
all of the necessary
ingredients for the building
and repair of our body
protein.

Note: Avoid the dairy
products which are high in
fats and therefore in
calories.

*If your meal lacks a complete protein (list B) then you should
mix the incomplete proteins (list A) so that between them they
provide complete protein. This basically means combining
pulses with either seeds or whole grains, for example:

soya beans/chickpeas/lentils/peanuts + rice/oats/wheat
beans/peas/lentils/peanuts + Brazils/sesame seeds.

Examples of these combinations can be found in the traditional
dishes of many different countries:

dhal (lentils) and chapatis (wheat) or rice — India
hummus (chickpeas and sesame seeds) — Middle East
baked beans on toast — England

. . . or Not to Eat (or Drink)?

List C — Foods to Avoid in Your Diet

White flour ⎫
White sugar ⎬ and their products e.g. bread, pastries, biscuits,
White rice ⎭ cakes jams and sweets.

these provide

Carbohydrate (processed)
Provides energy (calories) but it has had some of its nutrients removed and much of its fibre. Such food provides insufficient bulk, so often does not satisfy hunger and is more quickly digested and absorbed into the blood stream to raise blood sugar levels.

List D — Foods to Restrict in Your Diet

Oils ⎫
Butter ⎪
Margarine ⎬ in their obvious forms or
Cream ⎪ in prepared manufactured
High fat cheese — hard cheeses ⎭ foods.
  and cream cheese

these provide

Fats and Oils
These are very high in calories and in excess may be harmful to your body. They are present naturally in many foods (egg yolks, nuts and seeds) so will not be missing from your diet.

Note: Use very sparingly. Do not add to your cooking unnecessarily and use good non-stick cookware.

List E — Caution

Alcoholic drinks (lagers, beers, spirits, wines)

these provide

Alcohol and Carbohydrate
The amounts of alcohol and carbohydrate vary in different drinks but both provide calories and must be allowed for in the diet.

Special note for diabetics:
Special low carbohydrate lagers and beers are often stronger in alcohol and higher in calories. Many doctors think that ordinary beers etc. may be better in moderation, others question whether you should drink alcohol at all.

A Word About Sweeteners

Most sweeteners have a high calorie and carbohydrate content. Ideally then, both weight-watchers and diabetics try to exclude them from their diet wherever possible (although if you are a diabetic on insulin you should always carry glucose tablets or sweets with you in case of a hypoglycaemic attack). The trouble is, we tend to like sweet things even if we have reduced our sweet tooth! So, the pros and cons of ordinary sugar and alternatives, when you are desperate for some form of sweetener for desserts or baking, are discussed below.

Ordinary Sugar/Sucrose
(30g carbohydrate, 110 calories in 1 oz/25g)
White sugar — This is refined from sugar cane or beet. It is very concentrated and high in calories and carbohydrate. Sugar is quickly absorbed into the bloodstream to raise blood sugar levels (an obvious disadvantage for you if you are diabetic). Its contribution to dental decay is widely accepted.

Brown sugar — This is often used in wholefood cookery as
(raw)   a more healthy alternative to white. In fact,
                it is only marginally better containing minimal
                amounts of vitamins and minerals. It is still
                very high in carbohydrate and calories and
                will have the same effect on your blood sugar
                levels as the 'deadly white'.

**Using too much sugar uses up your carbohydrate and
calorie allowance and has an adverse effect on blood
sugar levels. Diabetics in particular take note.**

Molasses
(15g carbohydrate and 60 calories in 1 oz/25g)
                — This thick black syrup is left at the end of the
                sugar refining process, when all of the
                crystallized sugars have been removed from
                the raw sugar. It contains the vitamins and
                minerals originally present in the raw sugar,
                nevertheless it is still high in calories and
                carbohydrate. Used sparingly it would add a
                distinct flavour to cakes and biscuits and
                would contribute fewer calories and less
                carbohydrate than sugar.

Honey
(22g carbohydrate and 80 calories in 1 oz/25g)
                — Often regarded as another healthy alternative
                to white sugar it contains approximately 75
                per cent sugars, the rest being water with
                traces of vitamins and minerals. A little will
                add a distinct flavour — but use with care as
                it will still elevate the blood sugar.

Maple syrup
(25g carbohydrate and 100 calories in 1 oz/25g)
                — This is very concentrated. About 50 gallons
                (225 litres) of sap from the maple tree are
                needed to produce 1 gallon (4.5 litres) of
                maple syrup! It is high in calories and carbo-

hydrate so at the most add a slight dash (calculated) to your cooking to add a distinct flavour.

Malt
(23g carbohydrate and 105 calories in 1 oz/25g)

— This sticky brown syrup is produced from sprouted and toasted barley grains. It contains some vitamins a little protein and maltose sugar. Malt will add a distinct flavour to your cooking but can only be used sparingly because of its high carbohydrate and calorie content.

Fresh and dried fruit
(Variable carbohydrate and calorie content)

— Whole fruit with its natural fibre content requires digestion and this slows down the rate at which its sugars enter the blood stream. Fruit is rich in vitamins and minerals. Its bulk (especially fresh fruit) gives you that 'full up' feeling. Dried fruit as it is or soaked, adds sweetness to cakes and biscuits; fruit purée made from either fresh or dried fruit is great in bakes, desserts or as sauces or spreads. *Fruit is by far the best way to sweeten your dishes.*

Fruit juice
(Variable carbohydrate and calorie content)

— Juice has been extracted from the natural fibres of the fruit so it is more easily digested and can quickly raise blood sugar levels. It needs to be used sparingly but is preferable to sugar.

Fruit sugar/fructose
(30g carbohydrate and 100 calories in 1 oz/25g)

— Fructose is the fruit sugar, occurring naturally in many fruits. It is still a white refined sugar with the same amount of carbohydrate and calories as ordinary sugar. However it is 1 ½ times as sweet as ordinary sugar so you can use less. It is thought that it may cause a smaller increase in blood sugar levels than ordinary sugar. So, if you are diabetic, the British Diabetic Association recommend that 1 oz (25g) maximum can be taken in cooked dishes if spread throughout, the day, without counting the carbohydrate content in your allowance. However, it must generally be remembered that it is as high in calories as sugar. If you use fructose in cooking, you can halve the amount of sugar given in the recipe, but reducing the sugar content by as much as 1 oz (25g) may alter the results and a shorter cooking time may be necessary. Fructose has no flavour but does enhance the flavour of fruit and is sweeter with acid fruits and cold foods.

Fructose is preferable to ordinary sugar in your cooking: you will only need half the amount.

Aspartame
(Minute quantities needed so negligible calorie value)
— This is not a carbohydrate sweetener; it is composed of amino acids (the building blocks of proteins). It is 180-200 times sweeter than sucrose so very little is needed. However apart from being a sweetening agent, its use in cooking is limited at present.

Artificial sweeteners
— Just a mention here of these, since they are not natural and are not used in this book. Sorbitol is high in calories and although you do not have to worry about its carbohydrate content, it can have a laxative effect. Saccharine contains no carbohydrate or calories which is useful for diabetics but it does not appeal to the wholefooder.

Don't forget to make use of the different spices that emphasize sweetness, e.g., allspice, coriander, cinnamon, nutmeg, curry powder, mace, cloves.

Check List of Alternatives

Avoid or restrict these:	*Try these instead:*
white flour/bread/pastry/biscuits/pasta	wholemeal flour/bread/pastry/biscuits/pasta
white rice	brown rice
whole milk	skimmed, low fat milk
cream	natural yogurt/low fat soft cheese
high fat cheese	low/medium fat cheese
butter/margarine	low fat spreads/cheese
jams and marmalades	100% fruit jams/fruit purée
sugar	(fresh or dried) whole fruit (in desserts) or fructose if a sugar is essential (in baking)
lemonade etc.	sparkling mineral water
alcoholic drinks	no real substitute here: a small one now and again (unless advised differently by your doctor) should be alright

Wholemeal (from grains generally) or *wholewheat* (from wheat) flour is produced by grinding the whole grain. Brown (wheatmeal) flour, however has been partially processed so that some of the fibre and nutrients have been removed.

The Weight-watcher's Guide

If you are *diabetic* this page is not for you. If you need to lose weight you must first check with your dietitian regarding your carbohydrate and calorie allowance.

Surplus calories from any source, whether fats, proteins or carbohydrates can result in fat being stored in your body. Aim therefore to take in less energy (calories) than you are using up, whilst maintaining quality and balance in your diet.

Remember you will feel less hungry if you are eating unrefined foods because they contain more bulk.

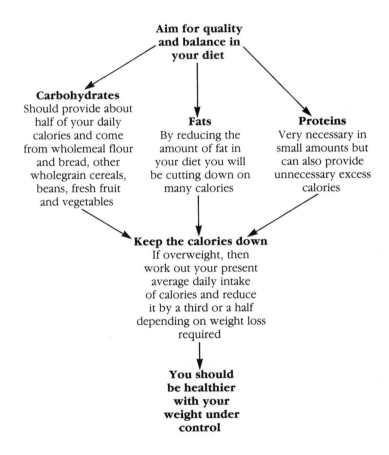

**Aim for quality
and balance in
your diet**

Carbohydrates
Should provide about
half of your daily
calories and come
from wholemeal flour
and bread, other
wholegrain cereals,
beans, fresh fruit
and vegetables

Fats
By reducing the
amount of fat in
your diet you will
be cutting down on
many calories

Proteins
Very necessary in
small amounts but
can also provide
unnecessary excess
calories

Keep the calories down
If overweight, then
work out your present
average daily intake
of calories and reduce
it by a third or a half
depending on weight loss
required

**You should
be healthier
with your
weight under
control**

The Diabetic's Guide

Diabetes is a very individual condition and needs individual help to control it. When it comes to food there are few rules that can be applied to all diabetics as different diabetics need different amounts of food for their particular life styles.

Basic rules

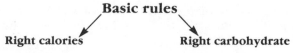

Right calories

1. Aim to maintain or achieve your ideal weight.

2. A maximum of one-third of your calories from fatty foods.

3. About half or more of your calories from carbohydrate.

4. Balance — have the same amount of calories each day.

Right carbohydrate

1. Use wholegrain fibre rich foods to make up your carbohydrate allowance.

2. Avoid fibre-free foods as much as possible.

3. Know your carbohydrate allowance for each meal.

4. Balance — have the same amount of carbohydrate each day.

If you are a new diabetic, then you must make sure that you inform your doctor or dietitian if you are following a vegetarian diet.

If you are an established diabetic and considering becoming vegetarian then you should consult your doctor or dietitian. Your diet will need to be reassessed and your carbohydrate allowance may be increased to ensure that all of your nutritional needs are met.

Correctly Calculating Carbohydrate and Calories

In the recipes, both the imperial and metric measures are given. However all of the carbohydrate and calorie calculations have been made on the imperial recipes and for the greatest accuracy the imperial system should be used. If the metric recipes are used the carbohydrate and calorie values given might be a little, but not significantly, out for an individual serving of say, a quarter of the dish.

In the 'Ways With Fruit and Vegetables' section, the idea of dividing fruit and vegetables into two groups — 'free' and 'counting' is explained. However, to obtain accurate carbohydrate and calorie values for the recipes, the contribution made by each of the ingredients has been included. By each recipe heading, the total carbohydrate content of the dish is given (to the nearest 5g) as well as its calorie content (to the nearest 10 calories). Ingredients with a significant carbohydrate content have been itemized to help make substitutions easier.

To calculate the carbohydrate and calorie value per serving, divide the totals given for each recipe by the number of servings. Most of the recipes will serve four people but it very much depends on how hungry everyone is and how many dishes make up the meal.

Balancing the Main Course and Dessert

A number of dishes in this book contain eggs in varying quantities, often to achieve a satisfactory bake, cake or rissole which is not too high in carbohydrate and which holds together. It is important to remember that egg yolks contain hidden fat, therefore it is not a good idea to rely on egg-containing dishes every day. Vary the diet with casseroles, stuffed vegetables, salads and other egg-free savoury and sweet dishes.

If the main course has a fairly high calorie content, then finish with a dessert such as fruit which will not add too many calories. If you are diabetic and watching carbohydrate as well as calorie content, then you will need to give a little thought in advance as to which main course and dessert, between them, will provide you with the correct intake. For example, if your allowance for the meal is 40g carbohydrate, then a main meal serving of 30g carbohydrate followed by a dessert portion containing 10g carbohydrate, would be fine.

(In this book the word carbohydrate has been abbreviated to *CHO* and calories to *cals.*)

1.

Ways with Fruit and Vegetables

Don't underestimate fruit and vegetables:

Eat a variety and combine them sensibly (see p. 11 for guidance on protein) and you will have all of the important nutrients in your diet.

Forget about the 'meat and two veg.' approach and desserts which are high in fat. Instead, think of animal products (milk, eggs, cheese, etc.) as the extras and let fruit and vegetables form the main part of your meal.

Important tips:

Buy fresh produce in season for a healthier and more economical diet.

Eat raw if possible, for the most nutrients.

Use as much of the fruit or vegetable as possible, leaving skins on where appropriate.

Don't cut them up smaller or sooner than is necessary. Some vitamins are destroyed by light and air or they leak out into the soaking water.

If cooking, cook to eat rather than save for leftovers to reheat (only 35-50 per cent of vitamin C originally present when first cooked, will be left).

The following tables will give you some idea of the fruit and vegetables which can be eaten fairly freely and the values of those which need to be allowed for. A more comprehensive and detailed list of food and values starts on page 179.

Free v Counting

When planning a meal or an accompaniment, fruit and vegetables can be divided into two broad groups:

'Free' — these can be eaten in moderate quantities without worrying too much about their calorie or carbohydrate content. (*Note:* their calorie and carbohydrate content *will* be included in the totals for the different recipes to give accurate calculations).

'Counters' — these need to be allowed for in your diet.

In time you will automatically know which foods are 'free' and the values of those which count.

Vegetables
'Free'

artichokes	cabbage	leeks	pumpkin
asparagus	carrots	lettuce	radishes
aubergines	cauliflower	marrow	runner beans
bamboo shoots	celery	mushrooms	spinach
beanshoots	chicory	parsley	swede
broccoli	courgettes	peas (fresh/	tomatoes
Brussels	cucumber	frozen)	turnips
(sprouts)	endive	peppers	watercress

'Counters' (for calorie and carbohydrate values, see page 179).

Beans/peas	lentils (dried)	brown rice	soya bean
(dried)	onions	sweetcorn	(dried)
broad beans	parsnips	water	
beetroot	potatoes	chestnuts	

Fruit
'Free'

gooseberries	lemons	redcurrants	rhubarb
loganberries			

'Counters' (for calorie and carbohydrate values see page 179).

apple	currants	melon	prunes
apricot	dates	orange	raisins
banana	fruit juice	peach	raspberries
blackberries	(unsweetened)	pear	strawberries
blackcurrants	grapefruit	pineapple	sultanas
cherries	grapes	plums	

Getting a Dish Together
When you are inventing a dish, be bold and adventurous because there are endless ways of presenting and combining fruit and vegetables.

Your final dish, hot or cold will depend on:
— which fruit and vegetables you prefer, whether they are in season and their cost, and perhaps, if they are to hand;
— whether the ingredients will complement the rest of the meal;
— the combination of flavours, colours and textures it is to achieve;
— its final carbohydrate and calorie content.

How large you make the dish will depend on:
— whether it forms all or only part of the course;
— the number of people you are feeding.

Start with the ingredients which you have got to allow for (if any) and decide on their quantities, then use the 'free' vegetables and fruit to complete the dish.

Ingredients for Salads and Hot Vegetable Dishes
These can be whole, grated, shredded, chopped, sliced, etc.
— most vegetables (raw or cooked and cold for salads, cooked and hot for other dishes);
— many fruits (raw or cooked);
— nuts and seeds (delicious toasted but remember the calories);
— wholemeal pasta (cooked);
— brown rice (cooked);
— herbs (fresh or dried — experiment with flavours);
— seasonings (peppers, mustard, garlic/celery salt, curry spices, etc.);
— salad dressings or hot sauces (pages 57 and 53 respectively) or better still invent your own.

Ingredients for Fruit Dishes
These can also be whole, halved, chopped, sliced etc.
— most fruits (fresh, dried or tinned in natural juice);
— nuts and seeds;
— fruit juice (unsweetened);
— spirits/dry apperitif or wine (occasionally);
— rose or orange flower water.

Some Salad Ideas
There are so many variations for salads and here are just a few suggestions.

Low Carbohydrate and Calorie Salads
(These salads can be eaten in moderate quantities without worrying too much about their calorie or carbohydrate content.)

Tomatoes +
onions

+ parsley + celery
+ watercress + beanshoots
+ cooked runner beans/french beans +
  courgettes (raw or cooked) +
  peppers
+ button mushrooms + peppers

White cabbage + onions	+ radishes
	+ parsley + peppers
	+ lettuce + watercress + chicory + cucumber
	+ tomatoes + mint

'Counting' Fruit and Vegetables Salads
(These salads include fruit and/or vegetables which need to be allowed for.)

Potatoes (cooked) + chives/onions	+ watercress + radishes
	+ celery + cooked cauliflower + runner/french beans
	+ oranges + cooked courgettes
	+ cooked peas + mint
Carrots + chives	+ sweetcorn + banana/pineapple + beanshoots + peppers + toasted almonds
	+ celery + apples + raisins + grapes + lettuce
	+ cabbage + apples + peppers
Beans (cooked) + onions	+ cooked cauliflower
	+ cabbage + dates + celery
	+ cooked brown rice + nuts
	+ wholewheat pasta, cooked + tomatoes
Brown rice (cooked) + spring onions	+ toasted peanuts
	+ mixed cooked vegetables
	+ cooked peas + oranges

Cooking Vegetables
You should cook vegetables for the minimum length of time.

Steam, grill, bake, casserole, sauté or stir-fry (in stock or soy sauce or yeast extract, not fat or oil). You will then retain the maximum nutrients and not be adding unnecessary fat. If you must boil vegetables then the best method is to stir the vegetables into the least amount of boiling water and keep the drained liquid for stock. *Never add* bicarbonate of soda.

When getting together a cooked mixed vegetable dish, cook the longer cooking vegetables first (e.g. onions, root vegetables, potatoes) and add the quicker cooking ones towards the end of the cooking time.

Cooked Vegetable Dishes — Variations on a Theme

Here is a suggested combination of vegetables which can form the basis for a number of recipes which often turn out quite differently.

COOKED VEGETABLE BASE
65gCHO, 500 cals. in total

2 lb (900g) lightly cooked vegetables e.g.,

½ lb (225g) cauliflower/broccoli/Brussels
½ lb (225g) carrots/turnip/swede
4 oz (100g) runner/french beans
4 oz (100g) peas (fresh/frozen)
4 oz (100g) courgettes
4 oz (100g) sweetcorn

2 medium onions, chopped
2 tomatoes, chopped
2 oz (50g) mushrooms, chopped

Sauté onions, tomatoes, and mushrooms in 1 teaspoonful yeast extract, 1 tablespoonful fresh chopped parsley and seasoning and then add to other vegetables.

Of course this base can be modified depending on vegetables preferred and available. This is a good way of tarting up leftovers!

With some of the following recipes using the above vegetable base, you do not need the vegetables ready cooked, e.g. when making a casserole or curry.

Recipes Using Vegetable Base

SPICED VEGETABLES
65gCHO, 500 cals. in total

Vegetable base (page 30) cooked or uncooked — see below (*65gCHO*)
1 tablespoonful curry powder or garam masala

1. If you are using cooked vegetables, then just stir them round with the spices in a wok or non-stick frypan until they are coated and heated through.

2. If you are using uncooked vegetables, slice or chop them finely and sauté them in the yeast extract and a little stock along with the spices.

VEGETABLE STEW OR CASSEROLE
70gCHO, 560 cals. in total

Vegetable base (page 30) (without the tomatoes) cooked or uncooked
— see below (*60gCHO*)
1 lb (450g) fresh tomatoes, skinned or 1 large tin (*10gCHO*)

Stew:

1. Either heat the cooked vegetables with the tomatoes for about 10 minutes.

2. Or, if starting from scratch, cook the vegetables with the tomatoes for about 40 minutes, adding the quick cooking vegetables towards the end.

Casserole:

1. Layer thinly sliced uncooked vegetables with the tomatoes in a dish. (If using tinned tomatoes, dissolve the yeast extract from the base, in the warmed tomato juice and pour over; if using fresh tomatoes, then dissolve the yeast extract in approx. 1 cupful of hot stock or water and pour over the vegetables.

2. Fit a tight lid and cook in the oven at 350°F/180°C (Gas Mark 4) for 35-40 minutes.

VEGETABLE CURRY
95gCHO, 640 cals. in total

Vegetable base (page 30) cooked or uncooked — see below (*65gCHO*)
1 pint (550ml) Curry sauce, pouring consistency (page 54) (*30gCHO*)

1. Either simmer the cooked vegetables in the prepared sauce for about 10 minutes, stirring to prevent sticking.

2. Or, if using uncooked vegetables, cook for 35-40 minutes in the sauce (to which the yeast extract from the base has been added).

CREAMED YOGURT VEGETABLES
115gCHO, 800 cals. in total

1 oz (25g) wholemeal flour (*20gCHO*)
3 small cartons natural yogurt (*30gCHO*)
Vegetable base (*65gCHO*) (page 30)
1 teaspoonful dried mixed herbs or 1 tablespoonful curry spices
Seasoning

1. Blend the flour with a little yogurt to make a smooth paste and then work in the rest of the yogurt.

2. Bring the yogurt slowly to the boil, add vegetables, herbs or spices and seasoning and bring back to the boil.

3. Cover and cook gently for about 10 minutes.

VEGETABLES AND PASTA
140gCHO, 860 cals. in total

Vegetable base (*65gCHO*) (page 30)
4 oz (100g) wholemeal pasta cooked (*75gCHO*)

Prepare using the method for Vegetables and Rice (page 33).

VEGETABLES AND RICE
155gCHO, 930 cals. in total

Vegetable base (*65gCHO*) (page 30)
4 oz (100g) brown rice cooked (*90gCHO*)

1. Mix all of the ingredients thoroughly, heating through quickly if necessary in a little soya sauce in a large saucepan or wok.

2. Garnish with chopped fresh herbs or tomato/cucumber slices.

VEGETABLES IN SAUCE
Variable CHO and calorie content

Vegetable base cooked or uncooked — (page 30) (*65gCHO*)
1 pint (550ml) pouring sauce (page 54)

1. Either pour the hot prepared sauce over the hot cooked vegetables, or;

2. If using uncooked vegetables, slice them thinly, layer in a dish (forget about the yeast extract in the base) and pour the prepared sauce over; fit a tight lid and cook at 350°F/180°C (Gas Mark 4) for 35-40 minutes.

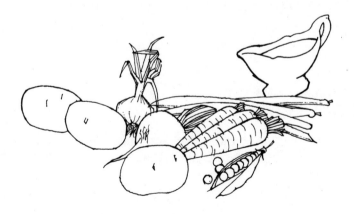

Toppings for Lightly Cooked Vegetables

A suggested base for these toppings is on page 30, although many other combinations of lightly cooked vegetables (approx. 2 lb/900g) would be suitable. A little vegetable stock can be added to the base if liked.

If the base is already hot, then a topping which can be grilled, provides a quick dish. If the base is cold, then the topped dish will need to be placed towards the top of a moderately hot oven 350°F/180°C (Gas Mark 4) to heat through and crisp the top.

Always remember to *add* the carbohydrate and calorie values of the toppings to those of the base to get the final value of the dish, e.g.,

	A dish comprising:	vegetable base	65gCHO	500 cals.
	and	bubble and squeak topping	95gCHO	490cals.
	contains:		160gCHO	990 cals.

(Herbs such as basil, marjoram, thyme, parsley, chives would be suitable for the following toppings.)

CHEESE AND NUT
Negligible CHO, 420 cals. in total   *Grill*

1. Mix 3 oz (75g) medium fat cheese, grated with 1 oz (25g) flaked nuts.

2. Sprinkle over hot vegetables and grill to brown.

EGG AND CHEESE
5gCHO, 360 cals. in total   *Grill*

1. Mix 3 oz (75g) medium fat cheese grated, with 1 egg beaten with 4 tablespoonsful liquid skimmed milk, herbs and seasonings.

2. Spread over the hot vegetables and grill to set and brown.

ONION AND COCONUT
10gCHO, 370 cals. in total   *Grill*

1. Sauté a large onion, chopped (*10gCHO*) with 2 oz (50g) desiccated coconut and mixed herbs in a little soy sauce until the onion is tender.

2. Top the hot vegetables and grill to crisp the onion.

COTTAGE CHEESE AND BREADCRUMBS
50gCHO, 360 cals. in total   *Oven/Grill*

1. Mix 4 oz (100g) fresh wholemeal breadcrumbs (*50gCHO*) with 4 oz (100g) plain cottage cheese, herbs and seasonings.

2. Top vegetables and brown the topping under the grill or at the top of the oven.

CRUMBLE TOPPING
75gCHO, 520 cals. in total   *Oven*

1. Mix 4 oz (100g) wholemeal flour (*75gCHO*) with 1 ½ oz (40g) low fat spread to form 'crumbs'.

2. Add seasonings and herbs.

3. Top vegetables and bake at 350°F/180°C (Gas Mark 4) until the topping is cooked and golden, about 20-25 minutes.

CRUNCHY OAT TOPPING
85gCHO, 520 cals. in total   *Oven/Grill*

1. Mix 4 oz (100g) regular oats (*85gCHO*) with 1 ½ oz (40g) melted low fat spread, herbs and seasonings.

2. Top vegetables and brown and crisp under the grill or at the top of the oven.

RICE AND CHEESE
90gCHO, 630 cals. in total   *Grill*

1. Mix ½ lb (225g) hot cooked brown rice (*90gCHO*) with 4 oz (100g) plain cottage cheese, herbs and seasonings, sprinkle 1 oz (25g) grated medium fat cheese on top.

2. Grill to brown.

POTATO TOPPING
95gCHO, 470 cals. in total   *Oven*

1. Mash 1 lb (450g) cooked potatoes (*90gCHO*) with 4 oz (100g) plain cottage cheese, chopped chives or spring onions and seasonings.

2. Top vegetables and place in a moderate oven for about 30 minutes until the top is brown and crisp.

BUBBLE AND SQUEAK TOPPING
95gCHO, 490 cals. in total   *Oven*

1. Add 4 oz (100g) cooked Brussels sprouts or cabbage, chopped to the potato topping above.

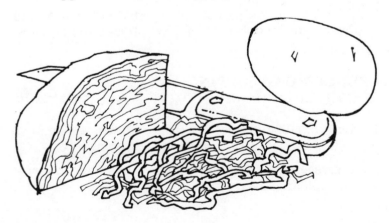

Cooked Stuffed Vegetables

Several vegetables are suitable for stuffing and provide delicious main dishes.

The filling, depending on what you include, will probably need to be counted and its carbohydrate and calorie value added to that of the shell. It is a good idea to start with either cooked brown rice (1 oz/25g contains *10gCHO, 55 cals.*) or fresh wholemeal breadcrumbs (1 oz/25g contains *12gCHO, 60 cals.*). To either of these you can add most vegetables (raw or cooked, grated, shredded or chopped); seeds or nuts, grated, ground or chopped; cottage, curd or grated medium fat cheese; herbs and seasonings. Use up leftovers this way.

Experiment with different combinations for the fillings and try them in different shells. Some examples are given later to help you.

Preparing and Cooking the Vegetable Shells
(Quantities for 4 people)

TOMATOES
4 large — 10gCHO, 50 cals. in total

1. Prepare as for peppers but bake at 420°F/220°C (Gas Mark 7) for 10 minutes.

PEPPERS
4 medium — 10gCHO, 70 cals. in total

1. Boil for a few minutes.

2. Cut off and keep the tops.

3. Remove the seeds and pith and discard.

4. Fill the peppers and replace the tops.

5. Cover with greaseproof paper and bake at 400°F/200°C (Gas Mark 6) for 30 minutes.

CABBAGE
2 lb/900g approx. — 10gCHO, 100 cals. in total

1. Boil whole in salted water for 10 minutes.

2. Cut off the top, scoop out the centre leaves and reserve for another dish.

3. Fill the hollowed cabbage and bake for 40 minutes at 400°F/200°C (Gas Mark 6) in a covered dish until tender.

COURGETTES
8 small/4 large — 20gCHO, 80 cals. in total

1. Cut in half lengthways and cut out a wedge in each half to form boat shapes; keep flesh for the filling.

2. Boil courgette halves for a few minutes (optional).

3. Fill halves with stuffing, cover with tin foil and bake at 400°F/200°C (Gas Mark 6) for about 35 minutes.

4. Remove foil towards the end to crisp the tops.

AUBERGINES
2 large/4 small — 20gCHO, 100 cals. in total

1. Boil for 2 minutes.

2. Cut in half lengthways, remove pulp and chop to use with stuffing.

3. Fill each half and bake for 1 hour at 300°F/150°C (Gas Mark 2).

MARROW
1 medium — 30gCHO, 140 cals. in total

1. Skin the marrow, cut in half lengthways, or cut into rings, or cut off one end.

2. Remove and discard centre, pith and seeds.

3. Fill the whole, the halves or the rings.

4. Cover with foil and bake at 400°F/200°C (Gas Mark 6) for 30 minutes or until tender.

In the next section there are some fillings for vegetable shells, but remember to add on their carbohydrate and calorie values.

If you find that you are a bit short of filling, then add ingredients, e.g., celery, cabbage, carrot, etc., which will not affect your calculations too much.

If you find that you have too much filling, then bake it separately in a small dish and serve with the stuffed vegetables so that your calculations for the meal still apply.

Some Vegetable Shell and Filling Combinations

Add the carbohydrate and calorie values of the fillings to those of the shells.

Mix all the ingredients together, including any flesh from the shell. Add seasonings.

Shell	Suggested Fillings for Shells
	Serves four

Aubergines (4) Filling
          40gCHO, 230 cals. in total
          1 medium onion, finely chopped
          1 each small red and green pepper, de-seeded and
            finely chopped
          1 oz (25g) sweetcorn
          2 oz (50g) fresh wholemeal breadcrumbs
          ½ teaspoonful dried mixed herbs
          2 teaspoonsful soy sauce

Courgettes (4) Filling
          50gCHO, 820 cals. in total
          1 medium onion, finely chopped
          2 oz (50g) almonds, ground
          ½ small carton natural yogurt
          3 oz (75g) fresh wholemeal breadcrumbs
          2 oz (50g) medium fat cheese, grated
          Pinch dried mixed herbs
          1 egg beaten

Tomatoes (4)   Filling
70gCHO, 550 cals. in total
2 oz (50g) brown rice, cooked
2 oz (50g) dried beans, soaked and cooked
4 oz (100g) mushrooms, chopped
2 oz (50g) medium fat cheese, grated
1 tablespoonful fresh parsley, chopped

Marrow (1)   Filling
70gCHO, 720 cals. in total
4 oz (100g) fresh wholemeal breadcrumbs
2 large carrots, grated
2 oz (50g) hazelnuts, ground
4 oz (100g) mushrooms, chopped
1 medium onion, finely chopped
1 teaspoonful dried mixed herbs
1 egg blended with 3 oz (75g) plain cottage cheese
   and juice ½ lemon

Cabbage (1)   Filling
110gCHO, 640 cals. in total
2 medium onions finely, chopped
4 oz (100g) brown rice, cooked
4 large tomatoes, skinned and chopped
3 tablespoonsful pine kernels, crushed and toasted
1 tablespoonful cider vinegar
2 teaspoonsful dried basil
½ clove garlic, crushed

Peppers (4)   Filling
130gCHO, 750 cals. in total
6 oz (175g) lentils, cooked
1 medium onion, finely chopped
2 oz (50g) mushrooms, chopped
4 oz (100g) celery, chopped
4 oz (100g) sweetcorn
½ carton natural yogurt
½ teaspoonful ground ginger
Dash soy sauce
1 tablespoonful tomato purée

More than a Baked Potato

Potatoes are cheap and very good value for money — they are nutritious, containing valuable vitamins and minerals.

They contain only 25 calories per ounce (25g) and 5g carbohydrate.

Baked potatoes in particular are very useful because:
— when cooking they need no fat and little effort;
— they are versatile, with many different toppings and fillings to choose from;
— topped or filled, and served with a salad, they can often provide a complete meal.

Baking Your Potatoes

1. Select 6 oz (175g) potatoes (*each 30gCHO, 150 cals.*) with good skins and uniform shape. Scrub well.

2. If topping your potatoes, then make a cross cut into the skin so that the potatoes open as they cook.

3. If filling the potatoes, prick them with a fork (if you want to halve the cooking time then push a clean metal rod or skewer through the centre of each one).

4. Bake the potatoes at 400°F/200°C (Gas Mark 6) for about 1 hour or until tender.

Toppings and Fillings
Quantities are for 4 potatoes

Suggested toppings are listed overleaf. You can also use them as fillers — just slice the top off the potatoes, scoop out the flesh, mix with the filling and pile back into the potato shells. Return to the oven for a few minutes if liked.

Add your own herbs and seasonings to these extras:

	gCHO	cals.
½ lb (225g) plain cottage cheese (grill topping)	3	220
½ lb (225g) curd cheese (grill topping)	negligible	320
4 oz (100g) peanut butter (grill topping)	20	650
4 oz (100g) tahini (grill topping)	20	650
6 oz (175g) medium fat cheese, grated, and 4 tomatoes, chopped (grill topping)	10	600
Mushrooms, beanshoots and onions, sautéed	negligible	30
½ lb (225g) chilli or baked beans	30	165
4 eggs scrambled (topping only)	negligible	320
2 eggs separated, 4 oz (100g) medium fat cheese, grated (mix beaten yolks, potato flesh and cheese. Fold in stiffly beaten whites, place filling in shells and return to oven for 30 minutes) (filling only)	negligible	500

Uncooked Stuffed Fruit

Fruit stuffed with a savoury or sweet filling

can be

a snack   an appetizer   a salad   a dessert

Many fruits provide excellent shells.

Fillings can be chopped, grated or shredded vegetables, fruit, nuts and mixed with a dressing e.g. yogurt or low fat cheese.

Mix and match different shells and fillings. This way you can have a stuffed fruit which is very low in calories and carbohydrate, or one which contributes significantly to your allowance.

Preparing the Fruit Shells
(Quantities for 4 people)

TOMATOES
4 large — 10gCHO, 50 cals. in total

1. Cut off the tops, cut out the pith and seeds and discard.

PEPPERS
4 medium — 10gCHO, 70 cals. in total

Prepare as for tomatoes.

GRAPEFRUITS
2 very large — 20gCHO, 90 cals. in total

1. Cut in half and remove flesh.

2. Use flesh in filling.

HONEYDEW MELON
1¾ lb/800g — 25gCHO, 100 cals. in total

1. Cut off top and scoop out flesh, as balls or spoonfuls.

2. Use flesh in filling.

ORANGES
4 large — 40gCHO, 160 cals. in total

Prepare as for grapefruits.

PEARS
4 medium — 40gCHO, 160 cals. in total

1. Prepare as for apples or halve, discard core and hollow out each half.

2. Use flesh for stuffing.

EATING APPLES
4 medium — 40gCHO, 160 cals. in total

1. Slice off the top, hollow out and discard core but chop flesh for the filling.
2. Coat flesh and inside of the shell with lemon juice.

Some Fruit Shell and Filling Combinations

Add the carbohydrate and calorie values of the fillings to those of the shells.

Mix all of the ingredients together including any flesh from the shell. Add seasonings.

If you find that you have insufficient filling, then just add some 'free' vegetables or fruit which will hardly affect your calculations. If on the other hand you find you have too much, then just serve separately.

Shell   **Filling Suggestions for Shells**
Serves four

Tomatoes (4)   Filling I
10gCHO, 60 cals. in total
½ small carton natural yogurt
1 celery stick, chopped
1 medium carrot, grated
1 spring onion, chopped
1 tablespoonful lemon juice

Filling II
20gCHO, 400 cals. in total
½ lb (225g) curd cheese
4 prunes, de-stoned and chopped
2 spring onions, chopped
½ teaspoonful dried basil

Oranges (4) Filling
10gCHO, 200 cals. in total
2 tablespoonsful red cabbage, shredded
1 celery stick, chopped
½ small carton natural yogurt
1 oz (25g) walnuts, chopped

Apples/pears Filling I
(4) *10gCHO, 260 cals. in total*
2 oz (50g) curd cheese
1 oz (25g) walnuts, chopped
1 celery stick, chopped
1 oz (25g) each black and green grapes, chopped

Filling II
20gCHO, 290 cals. in total
4 oz (100g) plain cottage cheese
1 oz (25g) raisins
1 oz (25g) hazelnuts, chopped and roasted

Grapefruits Filling
(2) *20gCHO, 80 cals. in total*
Flesh of 2 small oranges, chopped
½ honeydew melon flesh in balls
Fresh mint, chopped

Honeydew Filling
Melon (1) *25gCHO, 100 cals. in total*
1 small banana ⎫
1 small orange ⎬ all chopped
1 apple ⎭

Peppers (4) Filling
30gCHO, 310 cals. in total
5 oz (150g) beanshoots ⎫
1 small banana ⎬ all chopped
1 oz (25g) walnuts ⎭
2 large carrots, grated
1 small carton natural yogurt
2 tablespoonsful lemon juice

Fruit — Variation on a Theme

Here is a suggested combination of fruit which can be eaten as a fruit salad or can be used as a base for other recipes.

MIXED FRUIT BASE
80gCHO, 320 cals. in total

Alternatives which are fairly equal in their carbohydrate content are given on the same line — select according to preference or availability.

	gCHO	cals.
1 lb (450g) apples/oranges/pears/peaches/ plums/cherries	40	160
3 oz (75g) pineapple/grapes	10	40
2 oz (50g) peeled banana	10	40
6 oz (175g) raspberries/strawberries/ apricots	10	35
Juice of 1 very large grapefruit	10	45
Juice of 1 lemon	—	—
	80	320

Chop or slice the large fruit, and mix with the fruit juice which has been diluted with an equal quantity of water. Serve cold or heat gently on the top of the stove or in a covered dish in the oven.

Toppings for Fruit

The fruit base above can be used with the following toppings although approximately 1 ½ lb (675g) of most fruits, mixed or on their own would be fine. Some fruits, e.g. rhubarb, cooking apples and gooseberries will need to be cooked first and sweetened with fructose (1 oz/25g — *100 cals.*).

If the topping is just going to be grilled then the base must already be hot.

The carbohydrate and calories of the base and topping must be added together to give the final value of the dish.

The Crumble, the Crunchy Oat and the Cottage Cheese and Breadcrumb Toppings on page 35 can be used on a fruit base but omit the seasonings and herbs and add 1 oz (25g) fructose (100 cals.).

MERINGUE TOPPING
Negligible gCHO, 110 cals. in total   *Grill*

1. Whisk 2 eggs whites until stiff but not dry.

2. Whisk ½ oz (15g) fructose into the egg whites and fold in another ½ oz (15g) carefully.

3. Pile on to the hot fruit and grill for about 1 minute or until the top is golden.

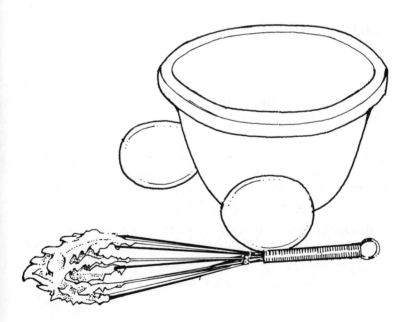

Alternatives with Fruit Purée

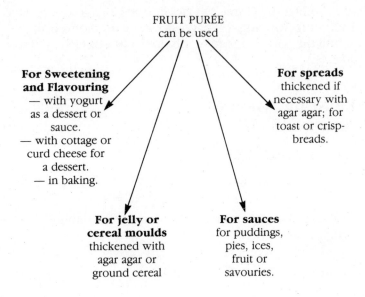

FRUIT PURÉE
can be used

**For Sweetening
and Flavouring**
— with yogurt
as a dessert or
sauce.
— with cottage or
curd cheese for
a dessert.
— in baking.

For spreads
thickened if
necessary with
agar agar; for
toast or crisp-
breads.

**For jelly or
cereal moulds**
thickened with
agar agar or
ground cereal

For sauces
for puddings,
pies, ices,
fruit or
savouries.

Making the Fruit Purée

1 lb (450g) fresh fruit or ½ lb (225g) dried fruit makes about ½ pint (275ml) purée.

The carbohydrate and calorie content of the purée will depend on the fruit which you choose (see page 27 for a quick check list).

Either you can rely on the natural sweetness of the fruit or add fructose (but remember the calories) or unsweetened fruit juice (¼ pint/150ml orange juice contains *15gCHO, 60 cals.*: ¼ pint/150ml apple juice *17gCHO, 70 cals.*).

Although you can purée or sieve the fruit, puréeing in a blender is preferable since you will not be discarding the fruit's fibre.

To purée fresh fruit:
    You can purée/sieve raw fruit which is already soft and ripe.

You can cook the fruit initially —
— juicy fruit such as berries and currants can be simmered in the very minimum amount of water or fruit juice until they form a pulp; sieve or purée;
— harder fruits such as pears and apples should be simmered in ⅓ pint/185ml water or fruit juice until tender; sieve or purée.

To purée dried fruit:
Soak fruit overnight in water or fruit juice (include in your calculations) with grated lemon rind.
Cook for about 30 minutes; purée or sieve.

To purée tinned fruit:
Use tinned fruit in natural juice; drain off some of the liquid and purée or sieve the contents.

Purée as a Sweetener or Flavouring

Added to natural yogurt (1 small carton, *10gCHO, 80 cals.*) it makes a dessert or a creamy sauce.

Blended with plain cottage cheese (4 oz/100g — *110 cals.*) or curd cheese (4 oz/100g — *160 cals.*) it makes a creamy dessert or ice-cream.

It can replace the liquid in recipes for cakes, biscuits and puddings, whilst sweetening at the same time.

Purée Jellies or Moulds

Purée can be used as it is or diluted with water or fruit juice.

Jelly: for 1 pint (550ml) purée, use 3 level teaspoonsful agar-agar (vegetarian setting agent). Sprinkle it carefully on to the hot purée and stir over the heat to dissolve and thicken. (Gelozone can be used instead of agar-agar but it has a stronger flavour; blend it first with a little cold liquid before adding to the hot purée). Pour into bowls to set.

Cereal Mould: for 1 pint (550ml) purée use 4 level tablespoonsful of ground cereal, e.g., brown rice flour, wholewheat semolina (approx. *40gCHO, 190 cals.*). Mix the cereal to a smooth paste with a little cold water. Heat the purée and pour on to the blended cereal, stirring well. Return to the heat and cook gently for up to 10 minutes to thicken, then pour into bowls to set.

Purée Sauces

Use purée as it is or diluted with water or fruit juice if necessary, to produce a pouring consistency. Serve hot or cold.

Purée Spreads

For 1 pint (550ml) purée use 2 teaspoonsful agar-agar or gelozone as described in the method for jellies above. Only make a few pounds of spread at a time as it will not keep as long as ordinary jam.

Put into hot clean jars and it will keep for about two weeks in the fridge. You can also store unopened jars in a freezer compartment but make sure that the contents have room to expand.

Finally — Some Good Fruit Combinations

Blackcurrants + oranges (flesh and grated rind)
Mixed berries/currants + grapes
Dried apricots + oranges
Dried apricots + pineapple
Strawberries + lemon (juice and grated rind)
Dried peaches + red currants
Gooseberries + oranges + banana + lemon (juice and grated rind)
Grapefruit + peaches + banana

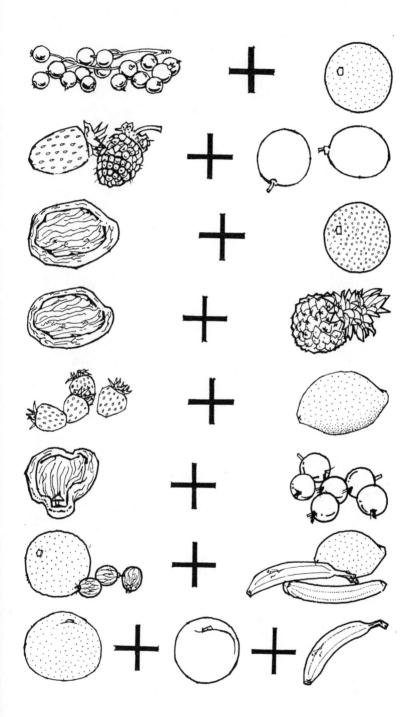

2.

Saucy Extras

Hot Sauces for Vegetable Dishes

A sauce, served separately, can provide a delicious addition to any main course or, if it is to be used as a coating, it can transform a bowl of vegetables into a far more exciting and unusual dish.

There are two main types of sauce in this section, both of which exclude fat or oil as an ingredient. The 'purée' sauce relies on vegetable purée to act as a thickener, whilst the 'thickened' sauce uses wholemeal flour to achieve a more solid, smoother consistency.

Ideas for Purée Sauces

(Ideally you will need a blender for these.)

TOMATO
10gCHO, 50 cals. in total

1. Purée 1 lb (450g) skinned tomatoes or 1 large tin tomatoes and add chopped onion, herbs (oregano or basil are good here) and seasoning.

2. Simmer to evaporate some of the liquid.

PEPPER
10gCHO, 60 cals. in total

1. Add a chopped red or green pepper to the Tomato Sauce before simmering.

MUSHROOM/CELERY/BRUSSEL
20gCHO, 250 cals. in total

1. Cook lightly 1 lb (450g) vegetables in ½ pint (275ml) liquid skimmed milk (*15gCHO*) with seasoning and herbs (chopped onion is optional).

2. Purée with 4 oz (100g) plain cottage cheese and gently heat — *Do not boil.*

BEAN
25gCHO, 140 cals. in total

1. Purée 4 oz (100g) baked or chilli beans (*15gCHO*) with the tomatoes of the Tomato Sauce.

CURRY
25gCHO, 150 cals. in total

1. Add 1 tablespoonful curry powder to the bean sauce.

Ideas for Thickened Sauces
(*Add* together the carbohydrate and calorie values of the ingredients used.)

Basic Sauce:
Pouring Sauce: 1 oz (25g) wholemeal flour (*20gCHO, 90 cals.*)

and   1 pint (550ml) water/vegetable stock
or   1 pint (550ml) liquid skimmed milk (*30gCHO, 180 cals.*)

Coating Sauce: 2 oz (50g) wholemeal flour (*40gCHO, 180 cals.*)

and   1 pint (550ml) water/vegetable stock
or   1 pint (550ml) liquid skimmed milk (*30gCHO, 180 cals.*)

1. Mix the flour with a little of the cold liquid to form a paste.

2. Heat the remaining liquid and pour slowly onto the paste, stirring continuously.

3. Return the mixture to the pan and stir until thickened.

4. Add onion, herbs and seasonings to this basic mix to form a white sauce.

Variations on the Basic Thickened Sauce

Make the following substitutions or additions to the basic pouring or coating sauce and add on any extra carbohydrate or calories. Cook the sauce for a while longer after adding any extras.

CELERY
Adds negligible CHO and cals. in total

1. Lightly sauté chopped celery.
2. Purée and make up to 1 pint (550ml) with water or vegetable stock to form the liquid of the basic sauce.

PARSLEY
Adds negligible CHO and cals. in total

Add 6 tablespoonsful finely chopped fresh parsley to the basic sauce made with skimmed milk.

BROWN
Adds negligible CHO and cals. in total

Make the basic sauce with the vegetable stock and add yeast extract, herbs to taste.

MUSHROOM
Adds negligible CHO and 60 cals. in total

1. Purée 1 lb (450g) mushrooms which have been lightly sautéed and make up to 1 pint (550ml) with water or vegetable stock to form the liquid of the basic sauce.
2. Add 1 teaspoonful yeast extract and 1 bay leaf to the sauce.

CHEESE
Adds no CHO and 260 cals. in total

Add 3 oz (75g) grated medium fat cheese to the basic sauce made with skimmed milk.

TOMATO
Adds 10gCHO, 50 cals. in total

1. Purée 1 lb (450g) skinned tomatoes or 1 large tin and make up to 1 pint (550ml) with water or vegetable stock, to form the liquid of the basic sauce.

2. Variations using Tomato Sauce:
   Curry (*adds negligible CHO and cals.*)
       Add 1 tablespoonful curry powder and a dash of lemon juice to the Tomato Sauce.
   Cheese and Tomato (*adds no CHO, 170 cals.*)
       Add 2 oz (50g) grated medium fat cheese to the Tomato Sauce.
   Chilli (*adds negligible CHO and cals.*)
       Add ½ teaspoonful chilli powder to the Tomato Sauce.
   Pepper (*adds 5gCHO, 30 cals.*)
       Add 1 each red and green pepper, finely chopped, together with a celery stalk finely chopped, to the Tomato Sauce.

PEANUT
Adds 10gCHO, 350 cals. in total

Add 2 oz (50g) crunchy peanut butter, the grated rind and juice of 1 lemon to the basic sauce made with vegetable stock.

YOGURT
Adds 30gCHO, 200 cals. in total

1. Use a large carton of natural yogurt instead of either stock or milk for the basic sauce.

2. Make a paste with the flour and a little of the cold yogurt.

3. Stir in the rest of the yogurt and mix well.

4. Gently heat the yogurt stirring until thickened.

Note: Try adding ½ small carton natural yogurt (*5gCHO, 35 cals.*) to any hot, but *not* boiling sauce to make it creamier, or dry wine (*1 tablespoonful negligible CHO, 10 cals.*) during cooking.

Some Dressings for Your Salads

With each of these dressings:
    Mix the ingredients well (a blender is very useful here but only blend those ingredients which are to be creamed or pulped to a smooth consistency, adding chopped herbs, fresh or dried, afterwards).

Experiment with seasonings, herbs (fresh or dried), flavourings (cucumber, peppers, onion).

Variations on a Yogurt Dressing

Add to   1 small carton natural yogurt (*10gCHO, 80 cals.*).

        2 tablespoonsful lemon juice;
  or 3 tablespoonsful fresh chives, chopped;
  or ½ teaspoonful curry powder, pinch each of ground cumin, pepper, dry mustard;
  or 1 small banana, mashed (*10gCHO, 40 cals.*), 2 teaspoonsful lemon juice;
  or 4 oz (100g) plain cottage cheese (*110 cals.*) sieved if not using a blender, 2 teaspoonsful lemon juice;

or 2 oz (50g) curd cheese (*80 cals.*), 1 teaspoonful
ground ginger, dash soy sauce, 1 teaspoonful lemon
juice, grated rind 1 lemon, 1 tablespoonful fresh
chives chopped;

or 3 teaspoonsful lemon juice, 1 tablespoonful roasted
sesame seeds (*negligible CHO, 50 cals.*),
1 teaspoonful caraway seeds, ½ teaspoonful
turmeric, pinch of ground nutmeg;

or 3½ tablespoonsful fresh horseradish grated,
1 teaspoonful made mustard;

or 2 tablespoonsful fresh mint chopped.

Variations on a Lemon Dressing

Add to   lemon juice.

fresh parsley or chives chopped;
or pinch dry mustard.

Variations on a Tomato Dressing

Add to   1 tablespoonful lemon juice.

4 oz (100g) plain cottage cheese (*110 cals.*) sieved
if not using a blender, 2 tomatoes chopped, spring
onion chopped;
or ½ pint (275ml) tomato juice (*10gCHO, 45 cals.*).

Fruit Sauces
See page 48 for ideas for fruit purée sauces.

3.

Soups

Basic Ingredients

— vegetables (these can include leftovers, or the tougher outside leaves, stalks etc.);
— stock (liquid from cooked vegetables or made with yeast or vegetable extract, soy sauce, miso, mushroom ketchup);
— seasoning (salt, pepper and spices);
— herbs (dried or chopped fresh) to include in the soup or for the garnish.

Extras

Ingredient	Amount	CHO/cal. count	Effect
— breadcrumbs, fresh, wholemeal	1 oz (25g)	*(12gCHO, 60 cals.)*	thickens
— cheese, medium fat, grated	1 oz (25g)	*(negligible CHO, 90 cals.)*	flavours
— lentils (dry)	1 oz (25g)	*(15gCHO, 85 cals.)*	thickens/ flavours
— nuts, toasted flaked	1 oz (25g)	*(negligible CHO, 150 cals.)*	garnishes
— Parmesan cheese	1 oz (25g)	*(negligible CHO, 115 cals.)*	garnishes
— peanut butter	1 oz (25g)	*(5gCHO, 165 cals.)*	flavours
— potato mashed	1 oz (25g)	*(12gCHO, 60 cals.)*	thickens
— sherry dry	1 tablespoonful	*(negligible CHO, 20 cals.)*	flavours
— watercress	few sprigs	*(negligible content)*	garnishes
— wine dry	1 tablespoonful	*(negligible CHO, 10 cals.)*	flavours
— yogurt, natural, (stir into hot but not boiling soup)	1 small carton	*(10gCHO, 80 cals.)*	adds flavour and creaminess

Simmer, never boil, soups.

Starter Soups of Negligible or Low Carbohydrate

(These soups would contain about *10gCHO* at the most when vegetables from the 'free' list on page 27 are used.)

CONSOMMÉ

1. Add 1 tablespoonful finely chopped or grated onion, a few cooked vegetables, yeast extract, seasonings and herbs to taste, to 2 pints (1.1 litres) vegetable stock.

2. Simmer for a few minutes to blend flavours.

CHUNKY

Cook 1 lb (450g) vegetables, sliced, diced, etc. with seasonings and herbs in 2 pints (1.1 litres) vegetable stock until tender.

PURÉE

1. Cook 1 lb (450g) vegetables in a little water until almost tender and then drain, reserving liquid to make it up to 1 pint (550ml) with water or vegetable stock.

2. Sieve vegetables or purée in a blender with a little of the liquid.

3. Combine purée and stock, add seasonings and herbs and simmer for a few minutes.

Starter Soups of Higher Carbohydrate and Calorie Content

CREAMY
40gCHO, 300 cals. in total

1. Prepare vegetable purée and stock as described in the purée soup, using only ¾ lb (350g) of 'free' vegetables.

2. Blend 1 tablespoonful wholemeal flour (*5gCHO*) in a little of the cold stock.

3. Add 2 oz (50g) dried skimmed milk powder (*30gCHO*) to the rest of the stock and heat gently.

4. Slowly add the hot liquid to the blended flour and return to the heat.

5. Add the vegetable purée, herbs seasoning and simmer, stirring until thickened.

Counting Vegetable Soups

1. Use any of the previous soup recipes and include vegetables which count, e.g., potatoes, root vegetables and beans.

2. Allow for their carbohydrate and calorie content.

'Meals In Themselves' Soups

You can add additional root vegetables, potatoes, etc. to any of the previous soup recipes to provide hearty soups for meal replacements, but you will need to add up the final carbohydrate and calorie value of the soup.

Pulses (peas, beans and lentils) make filling and nourishing soups with a substantial calorie and carbohydrate content: they can therefore act as a main meal. Here are some sample recipes:

SPLIT PEA OR BEAN SOUP
130gCHO, 750 cals. in total

½ lb (225g) dried beans/split peas (*105gCHO*)
1½ pints (825ml) vegetable stock
1 large onion, finely chopped (*10gCHO*)
1 medium carrot, diced (*5gCHO*)
1 celery stick, chopped
Sprig parsley
Pinch each dried thyme, basil
Seasoning
1 lb (450g) fresh tomatoes or 1 large tin (*10gCHO*)

1. Soak the beans or peas overnight and drain.

2. Combine all of the ingredients except for the tomatoes and cook until tender.

3. Add the tomatoes and return to the heat before serving.

4. Purée for a smooth soup.

LENTIL AND TOMATO SOUP
150gCHO, 840 cals. in total

2 medium carrots, diced (*10gCHO*)
1 large onion, finely chopped (*10gCHO*)
½ lb (225g) red lentils (*120gCHO*)
2 pints (1.1 litres) vegetable stock
1 teaspoonful dried thyme
Seasoning
1 lb (450g) fresh tomatoes, skinned and chopped, or 1 large tin
   (*10gCHO*)

1. Combine all of the ingredients except for the tomatoes and cook gently for about 40 minutes or until the lentils are tender.

2. Add the tomatoes and cook for another 5 minutes.

3. Sieve or purée the soup in a blender (optional).

4. Re-heat and serve garnished with chopped fresh herbs.

Suggested Combinations for Soups

Carrots + celery + tomatoes + red peppers + chick peas +
   cinnamon + bay leaf
Carrots + cabbage + mixed herbs
Potato + leeks + bay leaf
Potato + watercress + marjoram
Lentils + carrot + lemon juice
Tomatoes + sweetcorn + bay leaf + thyme + marjoram + basil
Celery + almonds + marjoram
Green peas + lettuce + mixed herbs
Sweet potato + green pepper + tarragon
Broad beans + carrots + dry white wine
Parsnip + carrot + endive lettuce + basil
Asparagus + peas + marjoram + mint + thyme

Note: Onion may be added to any of these soups.

The following combinations contain only 'free' vegetables:
Courgettes + celery + basil
Tomatoes + celery + basil
Jerusalem artichokes + celery + bay leaf
Spinach + green peppers + tarragon
Mushrooms + peppers + tomatoes + oregano

4.

Appetizers and Savoury Snacks

Recipe	gCHO	calories	page
Hummus	80	1000	77
Pâtés			77
Green Pâté	negligible	50	77
Curd Cheese	negligible	500	78
Vegetable and Egg	20	580	78
Carrot and Walnut	20	660	79

This section is to help you with ideas for low or negligible carbohydrate starters for a meal and some of these are suitable to stave off hunger pangs in between meals.

Using Fruit

Uncooked stuffed fruit — see page 42.

Fruit Cocktails — some fruits can be soaked in water overnight and then liquidized, e.g.

BANANA AND APRICOT/PEACH COCKTAIL
70gCHO, 300 cals. in total

6 oz (175g) peeled banana (*30gCHO*)
3 oz (75g) dried apricots/peaches (*40gCHO*)
Lemon juice

1. Slice bananas and chop dried fruit.

2. Coat bananas in lemon juice and soak with dried fruit in 1 pint (550ml) water overnight and then liquidize.

3. Dilute if liked with more water or unsweetened fruit juice (provided it is counted) and serve in glasses with lemon slices on the rim.

FRESH FRUIT SALAD

Mix chopped/sliced fresh fruit with a little unsweetened fruit juice, allowing for any counting fruit or juice. Serve in glasses or on a bed of watercress or lettuce with fresh, chopped mint sprinkled over.

Using Vegetables

Many of the salad ideas on page 28 served on individual beds of lettuce or watercress, with a dressing, are a good way of getting the digestive juices flowing.

Here are some further possibilities to inspire you:

VEGETABLE STARTER
30gCHO, 180 cals. in total

1 large onion, sliced (*10gCHO*)
1 medium carrot, sliced (*5gCHO*)
2 large peppers, de-seeded and sliced (*5gCHO*)
4 oz (100g) cauliflower in small florets
1 lb (450g) tomatoes, skinned and quartered (*10gCHO*)
Juice 1 lemon
1 teaspoonful each dried oregano, ground coriander
Seasoning
Fresh herbs chopped to garnish

1. Put all of the ingredients except for the parsley, into a saucepan and simmer, covered, until the carrot is just tender. Shake frequently to prevent the vegetables scorching.

2. Serve hot or cold, garnished with the parsley.

RATATOUILLE
50gCHO, 260 cals. in total

2 large aubergines in 1 in. (2cm) slices (*20gCHO*)
2-3 courgettes in 1 in. (2cm) slices (*5gCHO*)
2 medium onions, thinly sliced (*10gCHO*)
1 lb (450g) tomatoes, skinned and halved (*10gCHO*)
2 large peppers, de-seeded and chopped coarsely (*5gCHO*)
1 clove garlic, crushed
1 teaspoonful dried basil
Seasoning

1. Combine all ingredients in a large casserole and simmer, covered, over a low heat for 20 minutes.

2. Continue to cook uncovered for another 15 minutes over a moderate heat.

3. Alternatively bake in a covered casserole dish at 350°F/180°C (Gas Mark 4) until the vegetables are tender, about 1 hour.

4. Serve hot or cold.

Note: For a minted version of this dish add 2 tablespoonsful fresh mint.

COURGETTE BAKE
50gCHO, 580 cals. in total

2 lb (900g) courgettes, trimmed and grated (*30gCHO*)
1 tablespoonful salt
4 eggs, beaten
2 small cartons natural yogurt (*20gCHO*)
Seasoning
Red pepper, chopped to garnish

1. Mix the courgettes with the salt, cover and leave to stand for about 1 hour.

2. Strain the courgettes and squeeze out the liquid.

3. Cook the courgettes in a large non-stick frying pan for about 5-10 minutes, until they are tender.

4. Drain off any surplus liquid.

5. Whisk together the eggs and yogurt and add to the courgettes and season.

6. Pour into a 2 lb (1 kilo) loaf tin and cover with lightly greased foil. Place in a dish and add water until it comes half way up the sides of the tin.

7. Bake for 1¼ hours at 350°F/180°C (Gas Mark 4) or until set, cooling in the tin for 10 minutes before turning out and garnishing with peppers.

Using Nuts and Seeds

Nuts and seeds are high in calories so reserve the following for either starting off a low calorie main course and dessert, or as snacks when the day's intake has been or will be, low in calories.

NUT OR SEED LOAF
10gCHO, 1000 cals. in total

4 oz (100g) toasted nuts, chopped, or toasted seeds (*5gCHO*)
½ lb (225g) curd cheese
2 celery sticks, finely chopped
2 tablespoonsful onion, grated
½ green pepper, de-seeded and finely chopped
Seasoning

1. Mix all the ingredients well, pile into a dish/tin lined with greaseproof paper, press down well and chill.

2. Turn out from the dish, remove paper and garnish with tomato or cucumber slices.

SPICY ALMONDS
10gCHO, 1280 cals. in total

4 tablespoonsful tomato juice
2 teaspoonsful each paprika, curry powder
Pinch cayenne pepper
Salt (ideally sesame salt)
½ lb (225g) almonds (*10gCHO*)

1. Mix together the tomato juice and spices and then stir into the almonds.

2. Spread the almonds on a tray and roast at 350°F/180°C (Gas Mark 4) for 10-15 minutes.

Note: Using peanuts instead of almonds will make the total value *20gCHO, 1300 cals.*

MIXED NUTS IN SESAME SALT
15gCHO, 840 cals. in total

2 oz (50g) each almonds/Brazils/hazelnuts (*10gCHO*)
2 oz (50g) peanuts (*5gCHO*)
2 tablespoonsful sesame salt (or 1 tablespoonful salt mixed with ground sesame seeds)

1. Sprinkle 1-2 tablespoonsful water over the nuts and coat well.

2. Add the sesame salt and mix well again.

3. Spread the nuts out on a baking tray and roast at 350°F/180°C (Gas Mark 4) for about 15 minutes.

TAMARI SUNFLOWER SEEDS
40gCHO, 1200 cals. in total

½ lb (225g) sunflower seeds (*40gCHO*)
2 dessertspoonsful soy sauce

1. Mix the seeds thoroughly with the soy sauce and spread out on a baking tray.

2. Toast them under a hot grill, shaking or stirring occasionally, for 5-10 minutes.

3. Cool and store in a sealed container.

Note: If you use peanuts in the above recipe, toast them for a little longer and they will contain *20gCHO, 1300 cals.*

Nut Balls

These do not require cooking, just mix all the ingredients together well, form into balls and coat in wheatgerm, sesame seeds or ground nuts.

CREAMY NUT BALLS
45gCHO, 920 cals. in total

4 oz (100g) curd cheese
4 oz (100g) chopped almonds/Brazils/walnuts (*5gCHO*)
3½ oz (90g) fresh wholemeal breadcrumbs (*40gCHO*)
1 tablespoonful tomato purée
½ teaspoonful yeast extract

1. Mix together all ingredients and form into balls.

NUT AND PARSLEY BALLS
55gCHO, 1460 cals. in total

4 oz (100g) ground almonds/Brazils/walnuts (*5gCHO*)
5 oz (150g) ground hazelnuts (*10gCHO*)
3½ oz (90g) fresh wholemeal breadcrumbs (*40gCHO*)
1 tablespoonful fresh parsley, chopped
½ teaspoonful yeast extract dissolved in 4 tablespoonsful hot water
Seasoning

1. Mix together all ingredients.

Using Yogurt and Cheese

You can use yogurt or a plain low fat soft cheese, or both, as the basis for your starter or snack and add a variety of extras, e.g. negligible carbohydrate and calorie vegetables and fruit, together with herbs and spices (coriander, ginger, cinnamon).

Serve on beds of lettuce or watercress and garnish with a sprinkle of paprika or tomato or lemon slices. You can use any of the yogurt dressings on page 57 (doubling the quantities to serve as a starter for 4 people) and mix with or pour over one or more of the following extras:

Negligible CHO and Calories:
Celery, chives, cucumber, onions, parsley, peppers, radishes and
  tomatoes

Negligible CHO but with Counting Calories:
1 oz (25g) almonds/Brazils/hazelnuts/walnuts, chopped
  (*160 cals. approx.*)
1 hard-boiled egg (*80 cals.*)

Counting CHO and Calories:
1 apple, grated (*10gCHO, 40 cals.*)
2 oz (50g) banana, chopped (*10gCHO, 40 cals.*)
1 large pear, chopped (*10gCHO, 40 cals.*)
7 oz (200g) melon, chopped (*10gCHO, 40 cals.*)
1 oz (25g) raisins/sultanas (*20gCHO, 75 cals.*)

Note: If you are just mixing the extras above with either yogurt or cottage cheese, then add their carbohydrate and calories together to get the total for the dish. Allow 1 small carton of natural yogurt per person — *10gCHO, 70 cals.*, or 4 oz (100g) plain cottage cheese — *negligible CHO, 110 cals.*

Two particularly nice yogurt dishes are:

CUCUMBER RAITA

20gCHO, 180 cals. in total

2 small cartons natural yogurt (*20gCHO*)
Pinch salt
½ teaspoonful paprika or chilli powder
½ teaspoonful ground cumin
1 teaspoonful fresh parsley or coriander leaves, chopped
1 cucumber, grated

1. Beat the seasonings into the yogurt and add the cucumber.

2. Chill before serving.

ONION RAITA

30gCHO, 200 cals. in total

2 small cartons natural yogurt (*20gCHO*)
2 medium onions, finely chopped (*10gCHO*)
1 tomato, chopped
½ in. (1cm) fresh ginger, chopped finely
1 tablespoonful fresh parsley or coriander leaves, chopped
Seasoning

1. Mix all of the ingredients very well.

2. Chill before serving.

Using Hard Cheeses

Keep to the medium fat hard cheese (1 oz/25g — *90 cals.*) rather than the high fat Cheddars etc. Cut into small cubes and mix with crunchy, crisp fruit and nuts.

CHILLED CHEESE RING
Negligible CHO, 880 cals. in total

½ lb (225g) medium fat cheese, grated
¼ cucumber, chopped finely
1 egg, hard-boiled and chopped
1 teaspoonful fresh chives, chopped
2 gherkins, chopped
½ teaspoonful made mustard
Dash soy/tabasco sauce
2 stuffed olives, chopped
1 teaspoonful lemon juice
Seasoning
2 oz (50g) curd cheese
Fresh parsley, chopped, to garnish

1. Mix all the ingredients together except for the parsley.

2. Shape into a firm roll and wrap in foil or greaseproof and chill in the fridge.

3. Serve sliced and garnished with parsley.

Crudités with Dips or Pâtés

Crudités are raw vegetables which you can use with either dips or pâtés. Even if you use counting vegetables, the quantities per person tend to be sufficiently small not to worry about. Wash and cut vegetables and then refrigerate in a polythene bag. Shake in lemon rind and juice just before serving.

Suggestions for crudités:

beetroot, raw, sticks
button mushrooms
carrot sticks/strips
cauliflower florets
celery sticks

cucumber sticks
parsnip sticks
pepper strips
radishes
spring onions

Dips and pâtés can be easily made using puréed vegetables,

soft cheese or grated cheese, yogurt, ground/chopped nuts, lemon juice, seasonings, herbs, spices and possibly a little dry wine. The dips should have a creamy consistency whilst the pâtés need to be fairly solid (press into a container and chill in the fridge).

Ideas for Dips

AUBERGINE AND PEPPER
10gCHO, 75 cals. in total

2 small aubergines (*10gCHO*)
2 tablespoonsful lemon juice
2 tablespoonsful spring onion, minced
2 tablespoonsful green pepper, minced
2 tablespoonsful fresh parsley, chopped
Seasoning

1. Peel the aubergine and cut into ½ in. (1cm) cubes.

2. Steam until tender and mushy, drain off any liquid and mix well with the other ingredients.

3. Chill for at least an hour.

RADISH AND CHEESE
10gCHO, 240 cals. in total

1 small carton natural yogurt (*10gCHO*)
4 oz (100g) curd cheese
2 tablespoonsful radishes, finely chopped
2 tablespoonsful watercress/parsley finely chopped
1 tablespoonful lemon juice
Seasoning

1. Mix the yogurt slowly into the curd cheese.

2. Add the remaining ingredients, blend well and chill.

PEANUT
15gCHO, 450 cals. in total

1 small carton natural yogurt (*10gCHO*)
1 oz (25g) peanut butter (*5gCHO*)
2 oz (50g) medium fat cheese, grated
1 tablespoonful red pepper, chopped
1-2 teaspoonsful curry powder
Pinch each garlic salt and chilli powder
Dash lemon juice

1.   Mix all ingredients well and chill.

TAHINI
20gCHO, 650 cals. in total

4 oz (100g) tahini (*20gCHO*)
Juice of 2½ lemons
1 garlic clove, crushed
Fresh parsley, chopped
Sea salt

1.   Mix all ingredients well adding sufficient water to form a
     creamy consistency.

BEAN
60gCHO, 300 cals. in total

3 oz (75g) pinto beans, cooked and drained (*40gCHO*)
1 lb (450g) tomatoes, skinned and chopped (*10gCHO*)
1 large onion, finely grated (*10gCHO*)
Crushed garlic, ground cumin and chilli powder to taste
Sea salt

1.   Purée beans and tomatoes.

2.   Mix with remaining ingredients and chill.

HUMMUS
80gCHO, 1000 cals. in total

4 oz (100g) chick peas, cooked (*60gCHO*)
½ cupful lemon juice
½ garlic clove, crushed
4 oz (100g) tahini (*20gCHO*)
Seasoning
Fresh parsley and paprika to garnish

1. Purée peas with a little water and mix with the remaining ingredients reserving the parsley and paprika for garnishing, and chill.

Ideas for Pâtés

Serve with thin wholemeal toast/pitta bread/crispbread/crudités. To make a large stunning pâté, choose different coloured pâtés and press them as layers into a lined dish. Turn out to serve.

GREEN PÂTÉ
Negligible CHO, 50 cals. in total

½ cupful watercress, chopped
½ cupful radishes, chopped
2 cupful cucumber, chopped
½ cupful spinach or sprouts, chopped
Fresh chives
Seasoning

1. Blend all ingredients in a blender.
2. Press mixture into a lined dish and chill.

CURD CHEESE
Negligible CHO, 500 cals. in total

12 oz (350g) curd cheese
Fresh chives, chopped
Dash soy sauce
Peppers/tomatoes/cucumber, finely chopped
Seasoning

1. Mix all ingredients well.

2. Press into a lined dish and chill.

VEGETABLE AND EGG
20gCHO, 580 cals. in total

6 oz (175g) cooked green beans
2 tablespoonsful dry white wine
1 large onion, finely minced (*10gCHO*)
2 eggs hard-boiled, chopped
2 oz (50g) walnuts, ground
1 tablespoonful natural yogurt
Pinch ground nutmeg
Seasoning

1. Purée the beans with the wine.

2. Mix with the other ingredients, press into a lined dish and chill.

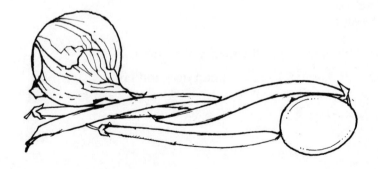

CARROT AND WALNUT
20gCHO, 660 cals. in total

2 medium carrots, finely grated (*10gCHO*)
4 oz (100g) walnuts, ground (*5gCHO*)
1 teaspoonful lemon juice
1 medium onion, finely chopped (*5gCHO*)
Fresh parsley, chopped
Seasoning

1. Mix all ingredients well.

2. Press into a lined dish and chill.

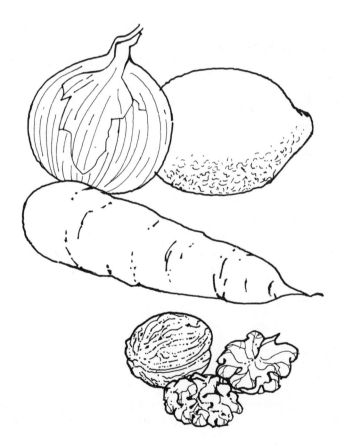

5.
Quick Meals

Some Time Saving Tips
Prepare more than you need of the following and keep the extra amount in a sealed container:

Nuts and seeds — ground, chopped, roasted.

Wholemeal breadcrumbs — keep in the fridge.

Hard cheese — grated, keep in the fridge.

Beans — soaked and cooked, keep in the fridge.

Brown rice — cooked, keep in the fridge.

Cooked vegetables — do not purposefully cook for tomorrow, but if there are leftovers, then keep them in the fridge and use them in quick dishes — rissoles, pancakes, omelettes, pitta bread, soups, stews, etc.

Useful Stores

Tinned tomatoes.

Tinned beans — these can change timetaking recipes into quickies (a large tin (15 oz/425g) can replace approx. 4 oz/100g dried beans in a recipe).

Frozen fruit and vegetables — those which come into the 'free' group are handy to make up the meal, whilst the 'counters' ensure (particularly if you are diabetic) that you have stand-by carbohydrate for the meal.

Wholemeal pitta bread — freezes well. Pop under a hot grill, heat both sides and either cut along one side lengthways and fill with vegetables, hot or cold, or cut in half crossways and fill each half.

Tinned fruit in natural juice — useful as a back-up and as a base for fruit salad.

100 per cent fruit jam — good for spreads, in yogurt or melted to make a sauce.

Cereal/fruit/nut snacks — muesli biscuits from Marks and Spencer; original crunchy bars by Jordans; Prewett's fruit bars etc. (values of these snacks and others can be found in the appendix under 'Manufactured Foods' on page 184).

Tins/packets prepared foods — made from soya protein etc.; nut mixes; bean dishes. (Manufacturers are usually happy to provide you with a nutritional analysis if we have not given it in the appendix of Manufactured Foods). Many of these can be used as a base for your own recipes.

Soy sauce, mushroom ketchup, tomato purée, peanut butter.

Useful Methods

Wash fruit and vegetables — when you have a spare moment, in advance of needing them (but do not leave soaking as you can lose valuable vitamins into the water); this will encourage the eating of proper meals rather than just snacks when you are short of time.

Pressure cook — rice, pulses, etc. to reduce cooking time.

Use a thermos flask — for automatic cooking. Just boil rice, small beans, lentils, etc. for 10 minutes, drain and then put them with fresh boiling water into the flask. Allow slightly longer cooking time than normal.

Make extra — rissoles, bakes, pancakes, etc. and freeze in containers marked with values of contents. (It is a good idea to freeze rissoles and pancakes by separating them with a layer of greaseproof paper.)

Main Courses

Recipe	gCHO	calories	page
Savouries			84
Cauliflower and Cottage Cheese Grill	negligible	400	84
Crunchy Egg and Vegetable Grill	60	900	85
Bean and Mushroom Savoury	70	520	86
Chilli Beans with Cauliflower	80	450	86
Mexican Beans	80	640	87
Corn Pudding	80	740	88
Onion and Cheese Oatie	85	700	88
Tomato Fritters	90	660	89
Speedy Pizza	90	780	90
Nutty Pasta	130	1200	91
Easy Two Bean Savoury	150	1300	92
Mushroom Spaghetti	170	880	93
Vegetable and Pasta Hot Pot	170	1300	94
Tagliatelle with Creamy Celery Sauce	235	1600	94
Rissoles etc.			95
Vegetable and Nut	30	480	96
Minted Pea	40	560	96
Broad Bean	60	360	97
Cauliflower and Potato	60	800	97
Oat and Walnut	60	1250	98
Root Vegetable	70	460	98
Mushroom and Cheese	70	720	98
Soya Bean and Peanut	75	900	99
Nut and Rice	70	1200	99
Peanut or Sesame	80	950	100
Vegetable	90	520	100
Potato, Cottage Cheese and Hazelnut	100	1050	100
Apple and Onion	120	720	101

There are some suggestions for getting together quick vegetable dishes in the 'Ways With Fruit and Vegetables' section. These include:

— salads;
— hot, quickly cooked mixed vegetables with rice, pasta or with soy sauce and spices added;
— vegetable base with a selection of grilled toppings;
— vegetables in different sauces;
— vegetable stew.

Some of the recipes in the 'When You Have The Time' main dish section could also be used when in rather a rush, if you have the necessary beans, rice or vegetables cooked already. (As a rough guide rice doubles its weight when cooked whereas pulses on the whole increase their weight two and a half times.)

   In this section are some more recipes worth having handy when you are trying to get a meal together in a limited amount of time.

Savouries

CAULIFLOWER AND COTTAGE CHEESE GRILL
Negligible CHO, 400 cals. in total

1 cauliflower
2 hard-boiled eggs, chopped
½ lb (225g) plain cottage cheese
Chopped chives/spring onions
Seasoning

1. Lightly cook the cauliflower.

2. Mash cauliflower and mix with the remaining ingredients, leaving half of the cottage cheese for the top.

3. Put under the grill to heat through and crisp off.

CRUNCHY EGG AND VEGETABLE GRILL
60gCHO, 900 cals. in total

1 medium onion, finely chopped (*5gCHO*)
2 celery sticks, sliced
1 medium carrot, finely sliced (*5gCHO*)
2 oz (50g) mushrooms, sliced
½ lb (225g) fresh/frozen beans
1 lb (450g) tomatoes, skinned and chopped (*10gCHO*)
⅔ pint (370ml) vegetable stock
2 oz (50g) wholemeal flour (*40gCHO*)
5 tablespoonsful liquid skimmed milk
Seasoning
1 tablespoonful lemon juice and lemon rind
4 hard-boiled eggs
1 oz (25g) medium fat cheese, grated
1 oz (25g) flaked almonds

1. Cook onions, celery, carrots, mushrooms, beans and tomatoes in a large non-stick frying pan for about 5-10 minutes.

2. Meanwhile add a little stock to the flour to form a paste.

3. Heat the rest of the stock and milk together and add to the blended flour.

4. Return the sauce to the heat, bring to the boil and add the vegetables.

5. Season and simmer for about 10 minutes, then add the lemon juice and rind.

6. Cut the eggs into quarters, arrange in a warm dish and pour over the vegetable/sauce mix.

7. Sprinkle the cheese and nuts on top and grill to brown.

Note: You can omit the eggs in the dish which will then contain only 600 cals.

BEAN AND MUSHROOM SAVOURY
70gCHO, 520 cals. in total

3 × 10 oz (275g) tins broad beans or 24 oz (675g) frozen/fresh,
  cooked (*60gCHO*)
1 oz (25g) medium fat cheese, grated
2 tablespoonsful lemon juice
4 oz (100g) mushrooms, chopped and lightly cooked
Seasoning
2 oz (50g) plain cottage cheese
1 oz (25g) fresh wholemeal breadcrumbs (*12gCHO*)

1. Purée or mash the beans (drain the tinned beans first).

2. Heat the beans in a non-stick pan with the cheese, juice,
   seasoning and mushrooms.

3. When the mixture is hot, top with the combined cottage
   cheese and breadcrumbs.

4. Grill to brown the top.

CHILLI BEANS WITH CAULIFLOWER
80gCHO, 450 cals. in total

1 medium cauliflower
1 large onion, chopped (*10gCHO*)
Yeast extract
2 tablespoonsful fresh parsley, chopped
1 large tin chilli beans (*60gCHO*)
Tomato slices to garnish

1. Lightly cook the cauliflower and drain.

2. Meanwhile sauté the onions in a little yeast extract until
   tender.

3. Add the cauliflower and beans and heat through.

4. Stir in the parsley and garnish the dish with the tomato slices.

Note: You can substitute sprouts, cabbage or broccoli for the cauliflower, and baked beans with added chilli powder for the tinned chilli beans.

MEXICAN BEANS
80gCHO, 640 cals. in total

1 lb (450g) cooked pinto beans (*75gCHO*)
2 tablespoonsful tomato purée
1 medium onion, grated (*5gCHO*)
1 teaspoonful dried mixed herbs/1 tablespoonful fresh herbs
2 oz (50g) medium fat cheese, grated
1 garlic clove, crushed
1 teaspoonful yeast extract
Seasoning

1. Purée or mash the beans and mix well with the other ingredients.

2. Fry the mixture in a non-stick pan until a thick paste is formed. These beans are great in hot wholemeal pitta bread, especially when chopped lettuce, onion and tomatoes are added.

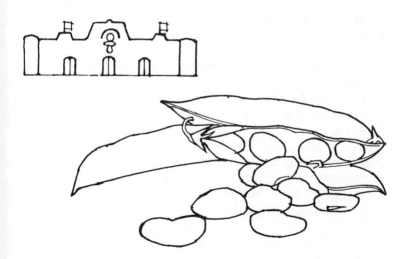

CORN PUDDING
80gCHO, 740 cals. in total

4 oz (100g) sweetcorn (*25gCHO*)
2 tablespoonsful natural yogurt
4 oz (100g) fresh wholemeal breadcrumbs (*50gCHO*)
4 eggs, beaten
½ red pepper, de-seeded and chopped
Seasoning

1. Mix all ingredients well.

2. Pre-heat the grill.

3. Meanwhile pour mix into a non-stick frying pan and cook for 6-8 minutes, lifting edges to allow the eggs to set.

4. When the underside is brown, place under the grill to brown and cook the top.

5. Serve in wedges.

Note: You can substitute peas, mushrooms, cooked potatoes, etc., for the sweetcorn, but you will need to alter the final value of the dish accordingly.

ONION AND CHEESE OATIE
85gCHO, 700 cals. in total

1 lb (450g) Spanish onions cut into rings (*25gCHO*)
3 celery sticks, finely sliced
2 medium carrots, grated (*10gCHO*)
1 small carton natural yogurt (*10gCHO*)
Seasoning
2 oz (50g) plain cottage cheese
2 oz (50g) medium fat cheese, grated
½ teaspoonful dry mustard
1 tablespoonful fresh/1 teaspoonful dried mixed herbs
2 oz (50g) rolled oats (*40gCHO*)

1. Cook onion rings in boiling, slightly salted water for 20-25 minutes and drain.

2. Add celery, carrots and place in a warmed dish.

3. Season the yogurt, warm gently and pour over the vegetables.

4. Mix cheese, mustard, herbs and oats and sprinkle over the vegetables.

5. Grill for about 5-10 minutes under a medium grill until the vegetables are heated through and the top brown.

TOMATO FRITTERS
90gCHO, 660 cals. in total

3 eggs beaten
½ pint (275ml) tomato juice (*10gCHO*)
Seasoning
8 small slices wholemeal bread, cut into triangles (*80gCHO*)
Fresh parsley, chopped to garnish

1. Mix eggs and tomato juice well and season.

2. Place the bread triangles in the tomato and egg mix and leave to soak.

3. When the bread has absorbed the liquid, fry the triangles on both sides in a non-stick frying pan to set the egg and to crisp.

4. Pile the triangles on a plate and garnish with the parsley.

SPEEDY PIZZA
90gCHO, 780 cals. in total

4 oz (100g) self-raising wholemeal flour (*75gCHO*)
½ teaspoonful sea salt
1 large onion, chopped finely (*10gCHO*)
1 teaspoonful dried oregano/basil
½ lb (225g) tomatoes, skinned and chopped (*5gCHO*)
Seasoning
4 oz (100g) medium fat cheese, grated

1. Mix the flour and the salt together and then add sufficient water (about 3-4 tablespoonsful) to form a stiff dough.

2. Press out into a 7 in. (18cm) round and fry in a non-stick frying pan for about 5-6 minutes.

3. Meanwhile prepare the topping by cooking the onions, herbs, tomatoes and seasonings together until the onions are tender and some of the liquid has evaporated.

4. Turn the dough over in the pan and spread the topping, alternately with the cheese, on to the base.

5. Cook in the pan for another 5-6 minutes, popping the pizza under a hot grill to get a bubbling topping, before serving.

Variation: To get an even quicker pizza, you can use wholemeal baps, each *25gCHO, 120 cals.*, cut in half and lightly toasted on both sides before adding the topping. Grill as above to brown the topping.

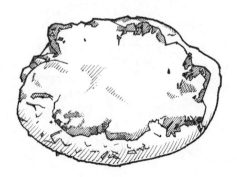

NUTTY PASTA
130gCHO, 1200 cals. in total

5 oz (150g) wholemeal macaroni/spaghetti (*95gCHO*)
1 lb (450g) tomatoes, puréed (*10gCHO*)
1 medium onion, finely chopped (*5gCHO*)
2 oz (50g) crunchy peanut butter (*10gCHO*)
1 teaspoonful soy sauce/yeast extract
2 each red and green peppers, de-seeded and sliced (*10gCHO*)
Seasoning
1 oz (25g) peanuts

1. Cook pasta in boiling salted water until just tender and drain.

2. Meanwhile, simmer puréed tomatoes, peanut butter, onion, soy sauce/yeast extract, peppers and seasoning for about 10 minutes.

3. Add cooked pasta and continue to simmer for a minute or two.

4. Serve garnished with peanuts.

EASY TWO BEAN SAVOURY
150gCHO, 1300 cals. in total

1 large tin red kidney beans (*60gCHO*)
1 large tin butter beans (*50gCHO*)
1 large onion, finely chopped (*10gCHO*)
Yeast extract
1 oz (25g) wholemeal flour (*20gCHO*)
1 large tin tomatoes (*10gCHO*)
½ teaspoonful dried oregano
Seasoning
2 tablespoonsful tomato purée
4 oz (100g) medium fat cheese, grated
1 oz (25g) walnuts, chopped
Fresh parsley, chopped to garnish

1. Drain both tins of beans.

2. Sauté the onion in a little yeast extract until tender.

3. Drain the tomatoes and use a little of the juice to mix with the flour to form a paste.

4. Heat the rest of the tomato juice, slowly add it to the blended flour and return to the heat.

5. Add the onions, beans, drained tomatoes, herbs, purée and seasoning.

6. Simmer the bean mixture, covered, for about 10 minutes and then spoon into a warmed dish.

7. Arrange the cheese in a line down the dish, sprinkling the nuts on top.

8. Place under a hot grill to melt the cheese and to brown the topping.

9. Garnish with the parsley.

MUSHROOM SPAGHETTI
170gCHO, 880 cals. in total

½ lb (225g) wholemeal spaghetti (*150gCHO*)
½ lb (225g) button mushrooms, chopped
2 medium onions, finely chopped (*10gCHO*)
1 lb (450g) fresh tomatoes, skinned and chopped
   or 1 large tin (*10gCHO*)
2 bay leaves
Seasoning

1. Cook spaghetti in salted water until just tender.

2. Meanwhile cook all of the other ingredients together for about 20 minutes, uncovered, to cook the onion and evaporate some of the liquid.

3. Remove the bay leaves.

4. Drain the spaghetti when cooked and mix with the mushroom sauce.

VEGETABLE AND PASTA HOT POT
170gCHO, 1300 cals. in total

4 oz (100g) wholemeal pasta (*75gCHO*)
1 pint (550ml) boiling water, salted
2 small courgettes, sliced
4 sticks celery, chopped
2 medium carrots, thinly sliced (*10gCHO*)
10 oz (275g) sweetcorn (*65gCHO*)
1/2 lb (225g) fresh/frozen peas (*10gCHO*)
1 teaspoonful chopped fresh ginger or 1/2 teaspoonful ground ginger
4 oz (100g) medium fat cheese, grated
1 small carton natural yogurt (*10gCHO*)
Seasoning
Fresh chives, chopped to garnish

1. Drop the pasta into boiling water, bring back to boil and cook for 5 minutes.

2. Stir in the courgettes, celery, carrots, corn, peas and ginger, bring to the boil again and simmer for 8 minutes or until the pasta is tender.

3. Remove from the heat and wait a short while before stirring in the cheese and yogurt. Season to taste.

4. Garnish with parsley before serving.

TAGLIATELLE WITH CREAMY CELERY SAUCE
235gCHO, 1600 cals. in total

12 oz (350g) wholemeal tagliatelle (*220gCHO*)
6 oz (175g) curd cheese
1 oz (25g) peanut butter (*5gCHO*)
1/3 pint (185ml) liquid skimmed milk (*10gCHO*)
4-5 sticks celery, finely chopped
Seasoning

1. Cook tagliatelle in salted water until tender.

2. Meanwhile blend the curd cheese with the peanut butter and then mix in the milk carefully.

3. Add celery to the creamy mixture and then heat gently in a saucepan.

4. Season the sauce and pour over the drained pasta.

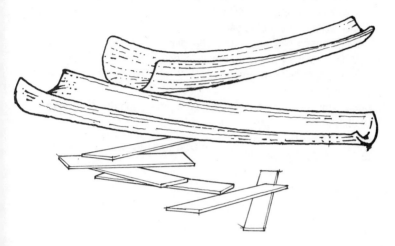

Quick Rissoles/Patties/Cutlets/Burgers etc.

To make these, you can use leftover (or planned extra), cooked brown rice or other whole grains (e.g., wheat, millet, barley, rye), potatoes, pulses or root vegetables; raw vegetables; onions; cereal flakes or flour; soya flour; ground or chopped nuts; herbs; grated medium fat cheese or low fat soft cheese; eggs; fresh wholemeal breadcrumbs.

Whichever ingredients you want to include, the method is basically the same — chopping/grating/mashing large pieces and mixing everything well, perhaps adding a little soy sauce or tomato juice/purée to moisten, as well as herbs to season and flavour. Form firm patties or whatever and coat in either natural bran, wheatgerm (1 oz/25g — *13gCHO, 100 cals.*), sesame seeds (1 oz/25g — *6gCHO, 160 cals.*) or fresh wholemeal breadcrumbs (1 oz/25g — *12gCHO, 60 cals.*).

You can either fry these burgers (without oil) in a non-stick frying pan over a low heat, or grill ensuring in both cases that they are cooked through without burning the outside. Ideally invent your own recipes, depending on the ingredients you have to hand and like. Meanwhile here are some to set the scene:

VEGETABLE AND NUT
30gCHO, 480 cals. in total

2 medium carrots, grated (*10gCHO*)
1 medium onion, grated (*5gCHO*)
2 sticks celery, finely chopped
2 tablespoonsful cabbage, finely chopped
1 oz (25g) fresh wholemeal breadcrumbs (*12gCHO*)
2½ oz (65g) hazelnuts, ground (*5gCHO*)
Pinch nutmeg
1 tablespoonful fresh herbs, chopped or 1 teaspoonful dried herbs
Seasoning
1 egg beaten
1 tablespoonful tomato purée } mixed together well

1. Mix all ingredients well.

MINTED PEA
40gCHO, 560 cals. in total

1 lb (450g) fresh/frozen peas, cooked (*20gCHO*)
1 medium onion (*5gCHO*)
1 teaspoonful dried marjoram
1 tablespoonful fresh mint, chopped
2 teaspoonsful lemon juice
3 oz (75g) soya flour (*15gCHO*)
Seasoning

1. Purée peas and onion and mix well with the other ingredients.

2. Cook well.

BROAD BEAN
60gCHO, 360 cals. in total

12 oz (350g) broad beans, frozen and cooked or tinned and drained (*25gCHO*)
2 medium onions, finely chopped/grated (*10gCHO*)
2 oz (50g) fresh wholemeal breadcrumbs (*25gCHO*)
2 tablespoonsful tomato purée
1 tablespoonful lemon juice
1 teaspoonful dried herbs (thyme, savory)
Seasoning, including curry spices if liked

1. Purée or mash beans and mix well with the other ingredients.

Note: If you substitute either cooked kidney/pinto/mung/aduki beans for the broad beans then the recipe will contain *85gCHO, 500 cals.*

CAULIFLOWER AND POTATO
60gCHO, 800 cals. in total

1 small cauliflower, cooked
4 oz (100g) cooked potatoes (*20gCHO*)
5 oz (150g) hazelnuts, ground (*10gCHO*)
2 oz (50g) fresh wholemeal breadcrumbs (*25gCHO*)
1 tablespoonful fresh parsley, chopped
1 medium onion, grated (*5gCHO*)
1 egg, beaten
1 teaspoonful garam masala
Seasoning

1. Mash cauliflower and potato and mix well with the other ingredients.

OAT AND WALNUT
60gCHO, 1250 cals. in total

6 oz (175g) walnuts, ground (*5gCHO*)
2 oz (50g) regular oats (*40gCHO*)
2 medium onions, finely chopped (*10gCHO*)
1 teaspoonful soy sauce
1 teaspoonful dried mixed herbs
1 egg, beaten
Seasoning

1. Mix all ingredients well.

ROOT VEGETABLE
70gCHO, 460 cals. in total

2 lb (900g) root vegetables, cooked (*40gCHO*)
2 oz (50g) fresh wholemeal breadcrumbs (*25gCHO*)
1 oz (25g) tahini (*5gCHO*)
Seasoning

1. Mash vegetables well.

2. Mix with breadcrumbs and tahini and seasoning.

MUSHROOM AND CHEESE
70gCHO, 720 cals. in total

4 oz (100g) medium fat cheese, grated
2 oz (50g) mushrooms, chopped
5 oz (150g) fresh wholemeal breadcrumbs (*60gCHO*)
1 large onion, grated (*10gCHO*)
1 egg white, whisked
1 teaspoonful dried mixed herbs
Pinch mustard powder
Seasoning

1. Mix all ingredients together well.

SOYA BEAN AND PEANUT
75gCHO, 900 cals. in total

12 oz (350g) cooked soya beans (*35gCHO*)
2 oz (50g) crunchy peanut butter (*10gCHO*)
2 oz (50g) fresh wholemeal breadcrumbs (*25gCHO*)
1 medium carrot, grated (*5gCHO*)
1 teaspoonful dried sage
Soy sauce to taste
Seasoning

1. Purée or mash beans.

2. Mix with the other ingredients.

NUT AND RICE
70gCHO, 1200 cals. in total

3 oz (75g) cooked brown rice (*30gCHO*)
1 medium onion, finely chopped (*5gCHO*)
5 oz (150g) hazelnuts, ground (*10gCHO*)
4 oz (100g) medium fat cheese, grated
2 oz (50g) fresh wholemeal breadcrumbs (*25gCHO*)
½ teaspoonful dried sage
Pinch nutmeg
Seasoning
1 egg, beaten

1. Mix all ingredients well.

PEANUT OR SESAME
80gCHO, 950 cals. in total

4 oz (100g) peanut butter or tahini (*20gCHO*)
4 oz (100g) fresh wholemeal breadcrumbs (*50gCHO*)
1 medium onion, chopped/grated (*5gCHO*)
1 medium carrot, grated (*5gCHO*)
1 tablespoonful fresh parsley, chopped
Seasoning

1. Mix all ingredients together well.

2. Add a little hot water if the mixture is too dry.

VEGETABLE
90gCHO, 520 cals. in total

1 lb (450g) fresh/frozen peas, cooked (*20gCHO*)
1 lb (450g) courgettes, cooked (*15gCHO*)
1 medium carrot, grated (*5gCHO*)
1 spring onion, chopped
4 oz (100g) fresh wholemeal breadcrumbs (*50gCHO*)
½ teaspoonful dried thyme
1 tablespoonful fresh parsley, chopped
Seasoning

1. Purée peas and courgettes.

2. Mix well with the other ingredients.

POTATO, COTTAGE CHEESE AND HAZELNUT
100gCHO, 1050 cals. in total

1 lb (450g) potatoes, cooked (*90gCHO*)
5 oz (150g) hazelnuts, ground (*10gCHO*)
4 oz (100g) plain cottage cheese
Spring onion, chopped
Seasoning

1. Mash the potato and mix with the other ingredients.

APPLE AND ONION
120gCHO, 720 cals. in total

2 medium onions, finely chopped/grated (*10gCHO*)
1 apple, grated (*10gCHO*)
1 celery stick, finely chopped
½ lb (225g) fresh wholemeal breadcrumbs (*100gCHO*)
1 egg, beaten
1 tablespoonful dried sage
Seasoning

1. Mix all ingredients well.

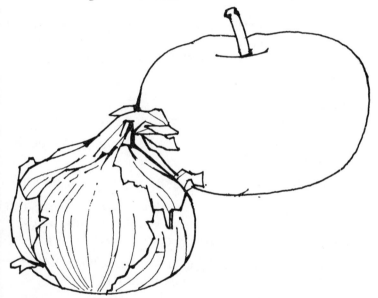

Omelettes, Pancakes and Their Fillings

Omelettes and pancakes can be savoury (ideas are in this section) or sweet (see page 117) depending on the extras. Just remember to add on the calories and carbohydrate of any additions.

You can add flavour either by adding extras to the basic mix or by using them as a filling when the omelettes or pancakes are cooked. Keep a note of the combinations you have tried and liked, together with the total value of the dish so that it does not need to be calculated again.

OMELETTES
Negligible CHO, 320 cals. in total

4 whole eggs
2 egg whites
Spices/herbs
Seasoning

Method One:

1. Beat eggs and egg whites with 4 tablespoonsful of water, seasonings, spices or herbs.

2. Add any extras to the basic mix.

3. Pouring a quarter of the mixture at a time into a hot, small non-stick frying pan, either cook in the usual way on one side, or you can turn the omelette over so that both sides are lightly browned.

Method Two:

1. Separate the yolks and whites of the whole eggs.

2. Beat yolks with any herbs spices or seasonings and add any extras for the basic mix.

3. Whisk all the egg whites until stiff and fold into the yolks.

4. Using a quarter of the mix at a time, pour into a hot small non-stick frying pan, cook the bottom of the omelette and then put under a hot grill to cook and set the top.

Note: In both methods, if you are adding a filling, fold the omelette over it and cook for a few more minutes.

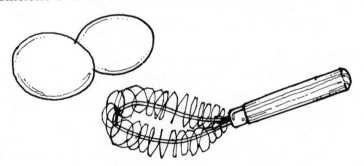

PANCAKES
90gCHO, 540 cals. in total

4 oz (100g) wholemeal flour (*75gCHO*)
Spices/seasonings/herbs
Sea salt
1 egg, beaten
½ pint (275ml) liquid skimmed milk (*15gCHO*)

1. Mix flour, seasonings and herbs and make a well in the centre.

2. Into the well, pour the beaten egg together with half of the milk, beating until smooth.

3. Add the remaining milk and mix well until blended.

4. Pour sufficient batter into a hot non-stick frying pan to coat the bottom when tilted.

5. Cook until the underside is brown and toss or turn to brown the other side.

6. Slide out of the pan and keep warm.

7. Repeat with the rest of the mix to make 8 pancakes.

8. Either roll up the pancakes with the filling inside, or tuck in the ends before rolling up to form parcels, or fold into quarters to form triangles.

9. Heat through and crisp, either at the top of a hot oven or under the grill.

10. Alternatively, layer the hot pancakes with the hot filling sandwiched between them.

Suggested Extras for Omelettes, Pancakes (and Hot Wholemeal Pitta Bread)

(Chop, slice or grate the ingredients as necessary.)

Negligible CHO and Calories:
Celery, chives, parsley, peppers, spring onion, spinach, tomatoes, watercress, lightly cooked beanshoots, cauliflower, courgettes, french beans, mushrooms.

Calorie Counters:
Almonds, toasted and flaked (1 oz/25g — *160 cals.*)
Cheese, cottage (1 oz/25g — *30 cals.*)
Cheese, curd (1 oz/25g — *40 cals.*)
Cheese, medium fat (1 oz/25g — *90 cals.*)
Peanuts, toasted and flaked (1 oz/25g — *160 cals.*)

Carbohydrate and Calorie Counters:
Apple (4 oz/100g — *10gCHO, 40 cals.*)
Beans, kidney, haricot, cooked (4 oz/100g — *20gCHO, 100 cals.*)
Brown rice, cooked (4 oz/100g — *40gCHO, 200 cals.*)
Peas, fresh/frozen, cooked (4 oz/100g — *5gCHO, 45 cals.*)
Pineapple (3 oz/75g — *10gCHO, 40 cals.*)
Potatoes, cooked (4 oz/100g — *20gCHO, 100 cals.*)
Sweetcorn cooked or tinned (4 oz/100g — *25gCHO, 140 cals.*)
Yogurt, natural (1 small carton — *10gCHO, 80 cals.*)

Some Filling Combinations for Omelettes and Pancakes

WATERCRESS AND MUSHROOM
10gCHO, 100 cals. in total

1 bunch watercress, chopped
½ lb (225g) button mushrooms, chopped
1 small carton natural yogurt (*10gCHO*)
Seasoning

1. Mix all ingredients well.

2. Warm through if liked.

APPLE AND CHEESE
10gCHO, 560 cals. in total

1 medium cooking apple, grated (*10gCHO*)
Lemon juice
1 celery stick, chopped
6 oz (175g) medium fat cheese in small cubes
1 level teaspoonful made mustard
Seasoning

1. Coat apple with lemon juice.

2. Mix apple with the remaining ingredients.

MUSHROOM, PEAS AND ALMOND
20gCHO, 600 cals. in total

1 small carton natural yogurt (*10gCHO*)
2 oz (50g) curd cheese
½ lb (225g) button mushrooms, chopped
½ lb (225g) fresh/frozen peas, cooked (*10gCHO*)
2 oz (50g) almonds, toasted and flaked
Pinch nutmeg
Seasoning

1. Carefully blend yogurt into the cheese.

2. Mix the cheese/yogurt into the other ingredients and gently heat through.

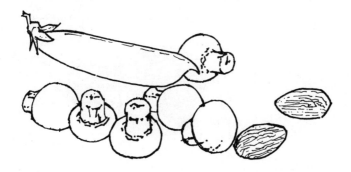

CHINESE VEGETABLE
30gCHO, 120 cals. in total

½ lb (225g) beanshoots
1 medium onion, finely chopped (*5gCHO*)
1 red pepper, de-seeded and chopped
4 oz (100g) fresh/frozen peas, cooked (*5gCHO*)
4 oz (100g) water chestnuts, chopped (*20gCHO*)
Soy sauce
Seasoning

1. Heat the vegetables through by stirring them in the soy sauce and seasonings.

AUBERGINE AND PEPPER
30gCHO, 320 cals. in total

2 small aubergines, skinned and chopped (*10gCHO*)
1 medium onion, chopped (*5gCHO*)
1 red pepper, de-seeded and chopped
1 courgette, chopped
½ teaspoonful dried mixed herbs
2 teaspoonsful soy sauce
Seasoning
1 oz (25g) fresh wholemeal breadcrumbs (*12gCHO*)
4 oz (100g) curd cheese

1. Cook the vegetables and herbs in the soy sauce and seasonings until tender.

2. Add the breadcrumbs and curd cheese and mix well.

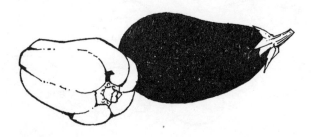

CREAMY SPINACH
40gCHO, 550 cals. in total

1 lb (450g) cooked spinach/2 lb (900g) raw weight (*30gCHO*)
1 large onion, chopped finely (*10gCHO*)
2 oz (50g) curd cheese
2 oz (50g) Parmesan cheese
Pinch nutmeg
Seasoning

1. Drain the spinach well and chop.

2. Mix spinach with the other ingredients.

CRISP VEGETABLE
50gCHO, 260 cals. in total

2 medium onions, chopped (*10gCHO*)
1 red pepper, de-seeded and chopped
1 lb (450g) cabbage, shredded
1 oz (25g) raisins (*20gCHO*)
1 apple, grated (*10gCHO*)
Seasoning
Fresh parsley, chopped

1. Stir all of the ingredients except for the parsley in a non-stick pan until heated through.

2. Add parsley at the end.

RATATOUILLE
50gCHO, 260 cals. in total

See page 68. This should be already prepared and added when hot with any surplus liquid drained off.

SPICED VEGETABLE
65gCHO, 500 cals. in total

See page 31. This should be prepared and added when hot.

MIXED VEGETABLE
80gCHO, 440 cals. in total

12 oz (350g) potato, cooked and mashed (*60gCHO*)
1 large onion, grated (*10gCHO*)
1 medium carrot, cooked and diced (*5gCHO*)
2 oz (50g) fresh/frozen peas, cooked
Juice ½ lemon
½ teaspoonful each ground ginger, coriander, mustard
Seasoning

1. Mix all the ingredients well.

2. For the omelettes and pitta bread the filling needs to be hot.

MEXICAN BEANS
80gCHO, 640 cals. in total

See page 87. These should be prepared and added when hot.

RICE AND NUT
100gCHO, 1060 cals. in total

½ lb (225g) brown rice, cooked (*80gCHO*)
1 medium onion, finely grated (*5gCHO*)
1 lb (450g) tomatoes, skinned and chopped (*10gCHO*)
4 oz (100g) walnuts, chopped (*5gCHO*)
Fresh parsley, chopped
Seasoning

1. Mix all the ingredients well.

2. Heat through gently if rice is cold.

Quicky Indian Recipes

In addition to the recipes below, some of those in the 'When You Have The Time' section can be prepared quite quickly if the beans or rice are already cooked.

Also see page 32 for Vegetable Curry; page 54 for Curry Sauce; page 31 for Spiced Vegetables.

FRESH CUCUMBER CHUTNEY
10gCHO, 70 cals. in total

1 cucumber, coarsely grated
1 each red and green pepper, de-seeded and finely chopped
2 cloves garlic, crushed
Spring onions, chopped
4 tablespoonsful lemon juice
1 teaspoonful fresh parsley, chopped
¼ teaspoonful cayenne pepper
Seasoning

1. Mix all the ingredients well.

TOMATO SALAD
20gCHO, 100 cals. in total

1 lb (450g) tomatoes, sliced (*10gCHO*)
1 large onion, grated (*10gCHO*)
Grated rind ½ lemon
1 tablespoonful fresh coriander leaves/parsley, chopped
½ teaspoonful black pepper
Good pinch each paprika, ground ginger, sea salt

1. Arrange tomatoes in a shallow dish.
2. Sprinkle the onion over the tomatoes, followed by the coriander or parsley, lemon rind and spices.

EGG CURRY (Anda ka kari)

20gCHO, 550 cals. in total

1 garlic clove
1 in. (2cm) piece ginger
½ teaspoonful chilli powder/paprika
1 teaspoonful coriander seeds
1 teaspoonful turmeric powder
½ teaspoonful cumin seeds
1 large onion, finely chopped (*10gCHO*)
1 lb (450g) tomatoes, skinned and chopped (*10gCHO*)
1 teaspoonful sea salt
2 tablespoonsful fresh coriander leaves/parsley, chopped
4 hard-boiled eggs, halved
1 teaspoonful garam masala
Lemon juice

1. Grind garlic, ginger and spices.

2. Put this paste, along with the onion, tomatoes, salt and coriander leaves into a pan and simmer gently until the sauce begins to thicken.

3. Add the eggs, sprinkle in the garam masala and heat through for about 5 minutes.

4. Add 1 tablespoonful lemon juice if liked before serving.

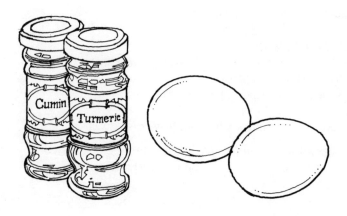

YOGURT CUTLETS (Dahi tikki)
100gCHO, 710 cals. in total

3 small cartons natural yogurt drained in a muslin, overnight
   (*30gCHO*)
2 oz (50g) wholemeal flour (*40gCHO*)
½ teaspoonful sea salt
½ teaspoonful paprika/chilli powder
1 teaspoonful garam masala
1 medium onion, finely chopped (*5gCHO*)
½ in. (1cm) piece ginger, finely chopped
½ oz (15g) pistachio nuts, chopped
1 oz (25g) almonds, chopped and toasted
1 oz (25g) sultanas (*20gCHO*)
2 oz (50g) fresh/frozen peas, cooked and mashed

1. Mix the drained yogurt with the flour, salt and spices.

2. Divide into 8 portions.

3. Cook onion in a non-stick pan until tender. Add ginger, nuts and sultanas and cook for a few more minutes.

4. Make a depression in each yogurt portion and put in the filling of mashed peas, ginger, onions, nuts and sultanas. Close up and shape into round cakes.

5. Fry on both sides in a non-stick pan to cook through and brown slightly.

6. Serve with spicy stir-fried vegetables.

MUSHROOM CURRY (Khumbi ki kari)
110gCHO, 550 cals. in total

1 lb (450g) button mushrooms, chopped
1 lb (450g) potatoes, chopped (*90gCHO*)
2 medium onions, sliced (*10gCHO*)
1 lb (450g) tomatoes, skinned and sliced (*10gCHO*)
1 in. (2cm) ginger, finely chopped
1 tablespoonful fresh coriander leaves or parsley, chopped
1 teaspoonful turmeric powder
½ teaspoonful chilli powder/paprika
Sea salt
1 teaspoonful garam masala
1 tablespoonful lemon juice

1. Cook everything in a covered pan except for the garam masala and lemon juice.

2. When the potatoes are tender, stir in the lemon juice and garam masala before serving.

SPICED POTATO SALAD (Alu raita)
120gCHO, 520 cals. in total

1 lb (450g) potatoes, cooked (*90gCHO*)
½ lb (225g) tomatoes, sliced (*5gCHO*)
2 small cartons natural yogurt (*20gCHO*)
½ teaspoonful cumin powder or seeds
Pinch chilli powder
Pinch black pepper
Sea salt
Fresh coriander leaves/parsley, chopped

1. Slice potatoes and mix with the tomatoes.

2. Beat yogurt with the cumin, salt and pepper and pour over the vegetables.

3. Garnish with the chilli powder and coriander.

(See page 73 for Cucumber Raita.)

Desserts

Recipe	gCHO	calories	page
Cereals			113
Hot Cereal Dessert	80	420	114
Christopher's Muesli (6 oz/175g)	80	580	115
Yogurt and Low Fat Cheese			116
Indian Yogurt	30	400	116
Mousse	35	240	116
Fruit Cream	35	420	117
Fruit Fool	40	220	117
Omelette, plain	*negligible*	320	117
Pancakes, plain	90	540	117

Fruit

Fruit is a good dessert to follow a substantial main course which has already provided you with complete protein. The carbohydrate and calorie values of the dish will depend on the fruit you use (see page 27 for a check list of free and counting fruit). You can serve fruit:

— on its own or mixed (page 67 for suggested fruit salad);
— cold or hot (stewed, grilled, poached in fruit sauce);
— with a different fruit purée sauce (page 50) hot or cold;
— as a hot fruit base with a quick grilled topping (page 46);
— as a mousse (fold in 4 stiffly beaten egg whites (*40 cals.*) into 1 lb (450g) fruit purée (page 48) and serve immediately.

Cereals

A cereal dessert is ideal after a nut or bean main course, especially if this course lacked any dairy produce.

HOT CEREAL DESSERT
80gCHO, 420 cals. in total

2½ oz (65g) ground brown rice/fine oatmeal/wholewheat semolina
  (*50gCHO*)
1 pint (550ml) liquid skimmed milk (*30gCHO*)

1. Mix the cereal with a little cold milk to form a paste.

2. Heat the rest of the milk with ½ pint (275ml) water until boiling and add slowly to the blended cereal and return to the heat.

3. Bring back to the boil and simmer, stirring to prevent sticking, for up to 15 minutes to cook the cereal.

4. Select from the extras (one or more) at the end of this section, to add either during or at the end of the cooking period. Just remember to add on any extra carbohydrate or calories.

Muesli

— this is a mixture of cereals, fruit, nuts and seeds;
— it can act as a breakfast, dessert, snack or topping;
— make up your own, calculating as you go, or use this one.

CHRISTOPHER'S MUESLI

Ingredients — select from each line and chop the large pieces	Quantity for 12 oz/350g	Quantity for 3 lb/1350g
Jumbo oats/muesli base	5 oz /150g (100gCHO)	20 oz/550g (400gCHO)
Dried apricots/apples/peaches	3 oz/75g (35gCHO)	12 oz/350g (140gCHO)
Raisins/sultanas/dates/currants	1 oz/25g (20gCHO)	4 oz/100g (80gCHO)
Brazils/walnuts/almonds (roasted)	1 oz/25g (negligible CHO)	4 oz/100g (5gCHO)
Hazelnuts (roasted)	1 oz/25g (negligible CHO)	4 oz/100g (5gCHO)
Sunflower seeds (roasted)	1 oz/25g (5gCHO)	4 oz/100g (20gCHO)
Total gCHO, in each batch	160gCHO	650gCHO

An individual serving of 1½ oz (40g) provides 20gCHO, 145cals.

To each serving you can add either ⅓ pint (185ml) liquid skimmed milk (10gCHO, 60 cals.) or 1 small carton natural yogurt (10gCHO, 70 cals.), or fresh fruit or unsweetened fruit juice (check values of fruit selected).

Yogurt and Low Fat Cheese

These provide complete protein, yet are quite light so serve them after a hefty cereal, nut or bean main course.

To natural yogurt you can add one or more of the extras in the list at the end of this section. Allow a small carton (*10gCHO, 70 cals.*) per person or 1 large tub (*30gCHO, 210 cals.*) would probably be sufficient for 4 people, especially if you are adding lots of extras.

Cottage or curd cheese blended with yogurt (add the yogurt slowly to the cheese, stirring to blend evenly) makes it more creamy or they can be used on their own to make a cool dessert.

INDIAN YOGURT
30gCHO, 400 cals. in total

3 small cartons natural yogurt (*30gCHO*)
1 dessertspoonful rosewater
½ oz (15g) chopped almonds, roasted
½ oz (15g) pistachio nuts, chopped
1 teaspoonful cardamom powder
Pinch each ground cloves, cinnamon powder
2 teaspoonsful fructose

1. Mix all ingredients well and chill.

MOUSSE
35gCHO, 240 cals. in total

½ lb (225g) soft fruit, puréed (*15gCHO*)
2 small cartons natural yogurt (*20gCHO*)
4 egg whites, stiffly beaten

1. Mix fruit purée with the yogurt.

2. Fold in the egg whites and serve immediately.

FRUIT CREAM
35gCHO, 420 cals. in total

½ lb (225g) soft fruit, puréed (*15gCHO*)
½ lb (225g) plain cottage cheese
2 small cartons natural yogurt (*20gCHO*)

1. Blend all ingredients well (sieve cottage cheese if not using a blender).
2. Chill before serving if possible.

FRUIT FOOL
40gCHO, 220 cals. approx. if using 'free' fruit

1 lb (450g) fruit, puréed (*15gCHO*)
2 small cartons natural yogurt (*20gCHO*)
Few sultanas (*5gCHO*)

1. Mix all ingredients well and chill if there is time.

OMELETTES
Negligible CHO, 320 cals. in total

The basic ingredients and method for making 4 omelettes are on page 102, just omit the salt and herbs. You can use the extras at the end of this section as fillings to achieve sweet omelettes but remember to add on any carbohydrate and calories.

PANCAKES
90gCHO, 540 cals. in total

Sweet pancakes, like omelettes, are a source of complete protein. They are also filling and therefore are good following a non-stodgy vegetable main course.

The ingredients and method to make a batch of 8 pancakes can be found on page 103. Omit herbs and seasonings and add any spices, essences, etc., to the batter mix. Extras for pancakes can be found at the end of this section. Experiment with combinations and quantities of the ingredients and the final appearance of the dish.

Depending on the filling, serve either with yogurt or a hot fruit purée sauce. (Remember to total the carbohydrate and calories). Crisp and heat the filled pancakes through under the grill. If fruit is the main ingredient for the pancake filling you will need about 1 lb (450g) for the eight pancakes; if curd or cottage cheese is the main ingredient you will need to use about 12 oz (350g) cheese.

Extras List

	approximate gCHO	cals.
4 oz (100g) apple/orange/peaches/pear/ plums	10	40
3 fl oz (75ml) apple juice unsweetened	10	40
2 oz (50g) apricots dried	25	100
8 oz (225g) apricots, fresh, whole	10	40
1 fl oz (25ml) brandy/whisky	negligible	65
1 oz (25g) Brazils/walnuts/almonds, roasted	negligible	160
4 oz (100g) plain cottage cheese	negligible	110
4 oz (100g) curd cheese	negligible	160
1 oz (25g) coconut (desiccated and roasted)	negligible	170
1 oz (25g) hazelnuts, roasted	negligible	110
4 fl oz (100ml) orange juice, unsweetened	10	40
3 oz (75g) pineapple	10	40
6 oz (175g) raspberries/strawberries	10	40
1 oz (25g) raisins/sultanas/dates/currants	20	70
2 fl oz (50ml) sherry dry	negligible	65
4 fl oz (100ml) wine dry	negligible	75

(Spices, lemon juice or rind, essences and the fruit on page 27 do not have to be allowed for.)

6.

When You Have The Time

Main Course

In the 'Ways With Fruit and Vegetables' section there are ideas for casseroles with various toppings, as well as stuffed vegetables and a selection of fillings. Here are some more recipes, some of which do not take very long to prepare if you remember to pre-heat the oven sufficiently early.

Savouries and Bakes

EASY CARROT AND CHEESE BAKE
50gCHO, 625 cals. in total

2 lb (900g) carrots, lightly cooked and mashed (*50gCHO*)
1 egg, beaten
4 oz (100g) medium fat cheese, grated
Chives/spring onions, chopped
Seasoning

1. Mix all ingredients well.

2. Press into a baking dish and bake in a moderate oven for about 20 minutes.

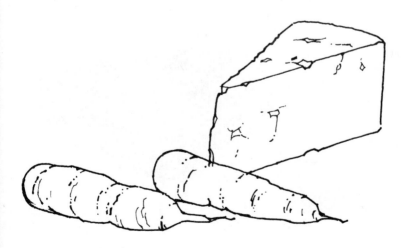

AUBERGINE, TOMATO AND YOGURT CASSEROLE
60gCHO, 440 cals. in total

2 large aubergines, sliced (*20gCHO*)
1 large onion, sliced (*10gCHO*)
1 lb (450g) fresh tomatoes, skinned and chopped, or 1 large tin,
   chopped (*10gCHO*)
1 tablespoonful tomato purée
1 teaspoonful dried oregano/basil
Seasoning
1 small carton natural yogurt (*10gCHO*)
1 oz (25g) Parmesan cheese
1 oz (25g) fresh wholemeal breadcrumbs (*12gCHO*)

1. Cook the aubergines in a non-stick pan until tender, drain
    and put aside.

2. Cook onions in the same pan until tender and stir in the
    tomatoes, herbs and seasoning. Simmer for about 5 minutes
    to reduce the tomato sauce.

3. Divide the aubergines into three and layer in a dish with
    the yogurt and tomato sauce.

4. Top with the breadcrumbs and cheese mixed together and
    bake at 350°F/180°C (Gas Mark 4) for 30 minutes.

WATERCRESS ROULADE WITH CHEESE AND TOMATO FILLING
60gCHO, 800 cals. in total

2 bunches watercress, trimmed
1 oz (25g) fresh parsley, chopped
2 oz (50g) wholemeal flour (*40gCHO*)
½ pint (275ml) liquid skimmed milk (*15gCHO*)
2 eggs, separated
2 large tomatoes, skinned and chopped (*5gCHO*)
½ lb (225g) cottage cheese
Seasoning

1. Place watercress in a pan with only the water clinging to the leaves from washing.

2. Cover and cook gently for 5 minutes, stirring occasionally. Drain.

3. Chop the watercress and mix with the parsley.

4. Make a paste with the flour using a little of the milk.

5. Heat the rest of the milk and slowly add to the paste. Return the sauce to the heat and cook for about 2 minutes, stirring to thicken.

6. Cool the sauce slightly and then beat the egg yolks into the sauce, together with the watercress, parsley and seasoning.

7. Fold in the stiffly beaten egg whites.

8. Spread the mixture over a non-stick Swiss roll tin and bake for about 20 minutes at 400°F/200°C (Gas Mark 6).

9. Turn the roulade out onto greaseproof paper, spread with the cheese tomatoes and seasoning, roll up and return to the oven for 5 minutes.

VEGETABLE AND NUT ROAST
60gCHO, 1100 cals. in total

1 medium onion, grated (*5gCHO*)
4 oz (100g) nuts, milled (*5gCHO*)
12 oz (350g) mushrooms/celery/cauliflower
4 oz (100g) fresh wholemeal breadcrumbs (*50gCHO*)
1 teaspoonful dried herbs
Seasoning
2 eggs, beaten

1. Lightly cook onion in a non-stick pan.

2. Meanwhile either sauté the vegetables (mushroom or celery) in their own juice, or steam/boil (cauliflower florets) to lightly cook.

3. Mix all the ingredients together, adding the eggs last.

4. Pile into a 1 lb (450g) loaf tin, cover with foil and bake at 375°F/190°C (Gas Mark 5) for 40-50 minutes or until firm.

MACARONI BAKE
60gCHO, 700 cals. in total

3 oz (75g) wholemeal macaroni, cooked (*55gCHO*)
3 oz (75g) medium fat cheese, grated
2 eggs, beaten
1 medium onion, chopped (*5gCHO*)
1 teaspoonful dried mixed herbs
Seasoning

1. Mix all ingredients well.

2. Bake in a 2 lb (1 kilo) non-stick loaf tin for 1 hour in a moderate oven at 350°F/180°C (Gas Mark 4).

RICE AND COTTAGE CHEESE PUDDING
70gCHO, 660 cals. in total

6 oz (175g) cooked brown rice (*60gCHO*)
½ lb (225g) plain cottage cheese, drained
2 celery sticks, chopped
2 tablespoonsful natural yogurt
1 tablespoonful lemon juice
2 spring onions, chopped
Parsley, chopped
1 egg, beaten

1. Mix all ingredients and bake at 350°F/180°C (Gas Mark 4) for 35-40 minutes or until set.

2. This dish can be browned off under the grill if liked.

NUT AND SEED MIX
70gCHO, 1300 cals. in total

1 teaspoonful yeast extract/soy sauce
4 oz (100g) fresh wholemeal breadcrumbs (*50gCHO*)
4 oz (100g) nuts, milled (*5gCHO*)
2 oz (50g) sunflower seeds, toasted (*10gCHO*)
1 medium onion, finely chopped/grated (*5gCHO*)
1 tablespoonful fresh chopped herbs/1 teaspoonful dried herbs
Seasoning

1. Mix the yeast extract with ¼ pint (150ml) hot water and stir into the breadcrumbs, leaving them to soak.

2. Combine the remaining ingredients and then add to the breadcrumbs, blending thoroughly.

3. Pile into a 1 lb (500g) loaf tin and bake at 375°F/190°C (Gas Mark 5) for about 40-45 minutes.

4. This mix can also be used as follows:
    — form into rissoles, coat with bran and bake (about 20 minutes at the top of a moderate oven) or fry in a non-stick pan;
    — to act as a filling for stuffed vegetables;
    — by adding extra vegetables, e.g. mushrooms, peppers, celery, tomatoes and a little stock if necessary, it can be used as a base for a shepherds pie or hot pot.

SPINACH AND CHEESE PIE
90gCHO, 1160 cals. in total

3 oz (75g) rolled oats (*60gCHO*)
4 oz (100g) medium fat cheese, grated
Seasoning
1 lb (450g) cooked (2 lb/900g raw weight) and drained spinach
  (*30gCHO*)
½ lb (225g) plain cottage cheese
2 eggs, beaten
Pinch nutmeg

1. Mix together the oats and grated cheese and seasoning.

2. Pack into the base of a non-stick baking tin.

3. Mix together the chopped spinach, cottage cheese, eggs, nutmeg and more seasoning.

4. Pile on to the base and bake at 350°F/180°C (Gas Mark 4) for 30-35 minutes.

CAULIFLOWER AND OAT BAKE
90gCHO, 750 cals. in total

1 medium onion, grated (*5gCHO*)
1 teaspoonful yeast extract
4 oz (100g) rolled oats (*80gCHO*)
2 oz (50g) button mushrooms, chopped
1 small cauliflower, broken into small florets and lightly cooked
2 eggs, separated
Seasoning
1 oz (25g) medium fat cheese, grated

1. Cook the onions in the yeast extract until tender.

2. Mix with the oats, mushrooms, cauliflower florets, beaten egg yolks and seasoning.

3. Stiffly beat the egg whites and fold into the vegetables.

4. Pile into a baking dish, top with cheese and bake at 375°F/190°C (Gas Mark 5) for 35-40 minutes.

VEGETABLE AND CURD CHEESE LOAF
100gCHO, 900 cals. in total

12 oz (350g) potatoes (*60gCHO*)
1 lb (450g) carrots (*25gCHO*)
4 oz (100g) frozen/fresh peas (*5gCHO*)
4 oz (100g) curd cheese
3 eggs, beaten
⅓ pint (185ml) liquid skimmed milk (*10gCHO*)
1 tablespoonful Parmesan cheese
1 teaspoonful dried mixed herbs
Seasoning

1. Cut potatoes and carrots into ½ in. (1cm) cubes and parboil with peas for a few minutes.

2. Beat the curd cheese until very soft and beat in eggs gradually.

3. Stir in the milk, Parmesan cheese, herbs and seasoning.

4. Place vegetables in a non-stick 2 lb (1 kilo) loaf tin and pour the cheese mixture over.

5. Cover with foil and bake at 375°F/190°C (Gas Mark 5) for 1 hour.

6. Serve hot or cold.

MUSHROOM AND COTTAGE CHEESE CRUMBLE
100gCHO, 900 cals. in total

1 medium onion, grated (*5gCHO*)
½ lb (225g) fresh wholemeal breadcrumbs (*95gCHO*)
6 oz (175g) plain cottage cheese
1 teaspoonful dried thyme
Seasoning
½ lb (225g) mushrooms, chopped
2 oz (50g) medium fat cheese, grated

1. Lightly cook the onion in a non-stick pan.

2. Add the onion to the rest of the ingredients, except for the mushrooms and cheese.

3. Place half of the crumb mixture in a dish, cover with the mushrooms and top with the remainder of the crumbs.

4. Sprinkle the grated cheese on top and bake for 30 minutes at 350°F/180°C (Gas Mark 4).

PINEAPPLE AND PEPPER ROAST
100gCHO, 1000 cals. in total

2 medium onions, finely chopped (*10gCHO*)
1 red pepper, de-seeded and chopped
4 rings pineapple, drained from natural juice, finely chopped (*20gCHO*)
2 oz (50g) almonds, roasted and chopped
2 tablespoonsful fresh parsley, chopped
6 oz (175g) fresh wholemeal breadcrumbs (*70gCHO*)
Rind 1 lemon, grated
1 teaspoonful dried thyme
Seasoning
2 eggs, beaten

1. Gently cook the onions in a non-stick pan until tender.

2. Mix with all of the other ingredients, adding the beaten eggs last.

3. Bake in a moderately hot oven, 375°F/190°C (Gas Mark 5), for about 35-40 minutes.

CHICK PEA AND NUT ROAST
100gCHO, 1250 cals. in total

4 oz (100g) chick peas soaked overnight (*55gCHO*)
2 medium onions, finely chopped (*10gCHO*)
1 tablespoonful tomato purée
2½ oz (65g) fresh wholemeal breadcrumbs (*30gCHO*)
4 oz (100g) nuts, ground (*5gCHO*)
1 teaspoonful dried sage
Seasoning
1 egg, beaten

1. Cook peas until quite tender, drain and mash with the remaining ingredients, adding the beaten eggs last.

2. Pile in to a dish and bake in a moderately hot oven 375°F/190°C (Gas Mark 5) for 30-40 minutes.

Note: Kidney, haricot, aduki beans can be substituted for the chick peas.

ROAST PEANUT AND RICE LOAF
100gCHO, 1350 cals. in total

4 oz (100g) peanuts, roasted and ground (*10gCHO*)
6 oz (175g) cooked brown rice (*60gCHO*)
1 medium carrot, grated (*5gCHO*)
1½ oz (40g) fresh wholemeal breadcrumbs (*20gCHO*)
2 medium tomatoes, chopped
1 medium onion, grated (*5gCHO*)
1 tablespoonful fresh parsley, chopped
Seasoning

1. Mix all of the ingredients together well and pack into a loaf tin.

2. Cover with foil and bake at 350°F/180°C (Gas Mark 4) for about 45 minutes, removing the foil after 30 minutes in order to brown the top.

3. This mix can also be used for rissoles which can then be coated with bran and baked or fried.

NUT AND CURD CHEESE BAKE
100gCHO, 2000 cals. in total

1 lb (450g) onions, finely chopped (*20gCHO*)
1 lb (450g) courgettes, sliced (*10gCHO*)
6 oz (175g) mushrooms, sliced
6 oz (175g) fresh wholemeal breadcrumbs (*70gCHO*)
12 oz (350g) curd cheese
2 oz (50g) almonds, toasted and chopped
2 oz (50g) walnuts, chopped
2 oz (50g) desiccated coconut
2 teaspoonsful tomato purée
½ teaspoonful each dried rosemary, sage, marjoram
Seasoning

1. Cook onions and courgettes in a non-stick pan until the onions are tender.

2. Add the mushrooms and continue to cook for another 1-2 minutes.

3. Combine with all of the remaining ingredients until evenly blended, pile into a dish and bake, covered, at 375°F/190°C (Gas Mark 5) for 40 minutes, removing the lid after 30 minutes in order to brown the top.

LENTIL AND MUSHROOM PIE
WITH CHEESE TOPPING
120gCHO, 720 cals. in total

6 oz (175g) red lentils (*90gCHO*)
½ pint (275ml) vegetable stock
Seasoning
Bay leaf
2 medium onions, finely chopped (*10gCHO*)
½ lb (225g) mushrooms, chopped
2 oz (50g) fresh wholemeal breadcrumbs (*25gCHO*)
1 teaspoonful dried mixed herbs/thyme/marjoram
1 oz (25g) medium fat cheese, grated

1. Cook the lentils in the vegetable stock with the seasoning and bay leaf until tender.

2. Drain off any surplus liquid from the lentils and remove the bay leaf.

3. Meanwhile cook the onions in a non-stick pan until tender, adding the mushrooms towards the end, again draining off any surplus liquid.

4. Mix the lentils with the mushrooms and onions, breadcrumbs and herbs.

5. Pile into a dish/tin and top with cheese.

6. Bake at 350°F/180°C (Gas Mark 4) for 30-40 minutes.

BEAN AND CORN BAKE
130gCHO, 720 cals. in total

10 oz (275g) cooked beans (*45gCHO*)
10 oz (275g) sweet corn (*65gCHO*)
1 teaspoonful dried mixed herbs
1 medium onion, sliced finely (*5gCHO*)
2 large tomatoes, sliced (*5gCHO*)
½ pint (275ml) tomato juice (*10gCHO*)
Seasoning

1. Place half of the beans in the bottom of a dish, followed by half of the corn and sprinkle herbs over.

2. Follow with a layer of tomato and onion.

3. Repeat these three layers again, finishing with the tomato and onion layer.

4. Mix the seasoning with the tomato juice and pour over the vegetables.

5. Bake for 40 minutes at 350°F/180°C (Gas Mark 4).

BEAN AND VEGETABLE LOAF
140gCHO, 900 cals. in total

10 oz (275g) haricot/kidney/aduki beans, soaked overnight
   (*125gCHO*)
1 medium onion, finely chopped (*5gCHO*)
2 medium carrots, grated (*10gCHO*)
1 egg, beaten
2 tablespoonsful fresh parsley, chopped
Seasoning

1. Cook beans until they are quite tender and drain.

2. Mash beans and mix with the remaining ingredients.

3. Pack into a loaf tin and cook, covered with foil at
    375°F/190°C (Gas Mark 5) for 40 minutes.

BARLEY, MUSHROOM AND PEA MIX
150gCHO, 760 cals. in total

6 oz (175g) pot barley (*135gCHO*)
1 pint (550ml) vegetable stock
4 oz (100g) fresh/frozen peas (*5gCHO*)
1 large onion, chopped (*10gCHO*)
2 vegetable stock cubes
Seasoning
1 lb (450g) button mushrooms

1. Heat the barley in a dry pan until toasted and golden.

2. Add stock to the barley, together with the onion, peas, stock
    cubes and seasoning. Cover.

3. Simmer very gently until the barley is soft, about 1 hour.

4. Towards the end of the cooking time, lightly poach the
    mushrooms in their own juice and add to the barley just
    before serving.

RICE AND BEAN BAKE
150gCHO, 800 cals. in total

4 oz (100g) brown rice (*85gCHO*)
4 oz (100g) dried beans, soaked overnight (*50gCHO*)
1 large onion, finely chopped (*10gCHO*)
1 medium carrot, grated (*5gCHO*)
2 oz (50g) button mushrooms, sliced
Fresh parsley, chopped
Pinch each dried rosemary and thyme
Seasoning

1. Cook rice and beans separately and then drain.

2. Lightly cook the onion in a non-stick pan and then mix all ingredients together.

3. Pile into a baking dish and cook, covered with foil for 20 minutes at 350°F/180°C (Gas Mark 4).

WHEAT CASSEROLE
160gCHO, 840 cals. in total

½ lb (225g) whole wheat, soaked overnight (*150gCHO*)
1 large onion, chopped (*10gCHO*)
4 celery sticks
2 medium tomatoes, skinned and chopped
7 fl oz (200ml) vegetable stock
2 tablespoonsful soy sauce
4 tablespoonsful fresh parsley, chopped

1. Cook wheat until just tender (about 1-1¼ hours).

2. Combine with the rest of the ingredients, place in a casserole dish and bake at 400°F/200°C (Gas Mark 6) for 30 minutes.

Note: 2 oz (50g) medium fat cheese, grated, can either be added to the dish and stirred in at the beginning or scattered on top towards the end of the cooking time. This will add *170 cals.*

LENTIL ROAST
180gCHO, 1100 cals. in total

½ lb (225g) red or green lentils (*120gCHO*)
1 lb (450g) onions, finely chopped/grated (*20gCHO*)
1 tablespoonful yeast extract
3 oz (75g) fresh wholemeal breadcrumbs (*35gCHO*)
2 oz (50g) tomato purée (*5gCHO*)
1 teaspoonful dried thyme/savory
Seasoning
1 egg, beaten

1. Cook the lentils until tender and drain.

2. Meanwhile cook the onions in the yeast extract until tender and then add to the remaining ingredients.

3. Bake in a 2 lb (1 kilo) loaf tin in a moderately hot oven 375°F/190°C (Gas Mark 5) for 30-40 minutes.

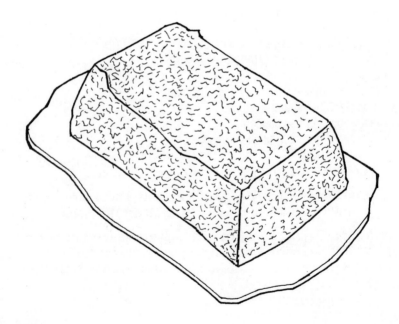

VERSATILE SAVOURY RICE
190gCHO, 1430 cals. in total

½ lb (225g) long grain brown rice (*175gCHO*)
1 red pepper, chopped
2 spring onions, chopped
2 oz (50g) sunflower seeds, toasted (*10gCHO*)
½ oz (15g) sesame seeds, toasted ⎱ (*5gCHO*)
1 oz (25g) pine kernels ⎰
Dash soy sauce
Seasoning

1. Cook the rice in ¾ pint (425ml) water until the rice is tender and all the water has been absorbed. (The best method of doing this is by placing the rice in cold water, bringing to the boil, turning the heat down, covering the pan and leaving the rice to simmer undisturbed for 30-40 minutes.)

2. Either mix the cooked rice immediately with the other ingredients and serve hot.

3. Or cool the rice and add to other ingredients and serve cold.

Note: If you use short grain rice in this recipe, you can make a mould by adding the other ingredients whilst the rice is still hot, pressing the mixture into a ring mould and refrigerating. When cold and set, turn out on to a plate and fill the hollow with watercress, tomato, slices of parsley, etc.

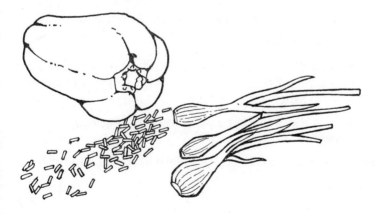

LASAGNE FLORENTINE
250gCHO, 1750 cals. in total

½ lb (225g) wholemeal lasagne (*150gCHO*)
1 medium onion, chopped (*5gCHO*)
1 lb (450g) fresh tomatoes, skinned and chopped, or 1 large tin, chopped (*10gCHO*)
2 teaspoonsful tomato purée
½ teaspoonful dried basil
Pinch dried thyme
Seasoning
2 oz (50g) wholemeal flour (*40gCHO*)
⅔ pint (370ml) liquid skimmed milk (*20gCHO*)
2 lb (900g) raw weight spinach, chopped and lightly steamed (*30gCHO*)
6 oz (175g) medium fat cheese, grated

1. Place the lasagne in a dish and pour boiling water over.

2. Place onion, tomatoes, purée, basil, thyme and seasoning in a pan, bring to the boil and simmer for 10 minutes.

3. Add a little of the milk to the flour to form a paste.

4. Heat the remainder of the milk and then add slowly to the flour paste.

5. Return the sauce to the heat, bring to the boil and cook, stirring for a few minutes to thicken.

6. Add seasoning and drained spinach to the sauce.

7. Drain the lasagne.

8. Spread a ⅓ of the spinach sauce on the bottom of a 3 pint (1.5 litres) oblong dish, cover with strips of lasagne, ⅓ tomato sauce and ⅓ cheese.

9. Repeat the layering twice more, finishing with a layer of cheese.

10. Bake at 350°F/180°C (Gas Mark 4) for 40 minutes.

LENTIL AND MILLET BAKE
260gCHO, 1950 cals. in total

½ lb (225g) red lentils (*120gCHO*)
½ lb (225g) millet, toasted (*130gCHO*)
1 large onion (*10gCHO*)
2 pints (1.1 litres) vegetable stock
2 oz (50g) nuts, ground
Fresh/dried herbs
1 tablespoonful yeast extract
Seasoning

1. Put lentils, millet and onion together with the stock into a large pan and bring to the boil.

2. Cover and cook over a gentle heat for 20-25 minutes until the lentils and millet are cooked and the water absorbed.

3. Add nuts, herbs, yeast extract and seasoning and bake at 375°F/190°C (Gas Mark 5) for about 30 minutes.

LENTIL AND POTATO HOT POT
275gCHO, 1360 cals. in total

½ lb (225g) red lentils (*120gCHO*)
1½ lb (675g) potatoes, sliced (*140gCHO*)
3 medium onions, sliced (*15gCHO*)
1 dessertspoonful yeast extract
¾ pint (425ml) vegetable stock
1 teaspoonful dried herbs
Seasoning

1. Put layers of lentils, sliced potatoes and onions in a dish, seasoning between the layers and finishing with the potatoes.

2. Dissolve the yeast extract in the warmed vegetable stock and pour over the vegetables.

3. Put the lid on the dish and bake at 400°F/200°C (Gas Mark 6) for 1 hour removing the lid towards the end to crisp the top.

Patties, Rissoles, Burgers, etc.

Most of these can be prepared fairly quickly with a little thinking ahead. If the necessary beans, rice, etc. are already cooked and the patties are fried in a non-stick pan or grilled instead of baked in the oven, then the preparation and cooking time just before the meal can be greatly reduced.

PINE NUT
50gCHO, 820 cals. in total

1 medium carrot, grated (*5gCHO*)
3 oz (75g) pine kernels, ground (*10gCHO*)
2 oz (50g) dry wholemeal breadcrumbs (*25gCHO*)
1 large onion, grated (*10gCHO*)
2 eggs, beaten
½ teaspoonful dried sage
Pinch celery seed (optional)
Seasoning

1. Mix all ingredients well.

2. Drop spoonsful on to a non-stick baking tray and bake for 15-20 minutes at 350°F/180°C (Gas Mark 4).

3. Brown under the grill.

LENTIL SAUSAGES
80gCHO, 720 cals. in total

4 oz (100g) red lentils (*60gCHO*)
½ pint (275ml) vegetable stock
2 oz (50g) medium fat cheese, grated
2 oz (50g) fresh wholemeal breadcrumbs (*25gCHO*)
½ green pepper, de-seeded and chopped
1 tablespoonful fresh parsley, chopped
Seasoning
1 egg, beaten
Natural bran to coat

1. Cook the lentils in the vegetable stock until tender and drain if necessary.

2. Mix together the lentils, cheese, breadcrumbs, pepper, parsley and seasoning.

3. Stir in the egg with the lentil mixture over a gentle heat and mix well.

4. Leave to cool on a wet plate.

5. Divide into 8, form sausages, coat in bran and bake at 375°F/190°C (Gas Mark 5) for 30 minutes.

CASHEW NUT
90gCHO, 1300 cals. in total

1 medium onion, chopped (*5gCHO*)
Yeast extract
1½ oz (40g) wholemeal flour (*30gCHO*)
⅓ pint (185ml) liquid skimmed milk (*10gCHO*)
5 oz (150g) cashew nuts, ground }
1 oz (25g) cashew nuts, chopped } (*45gCHO*)
2 teaspoonsful lemon juice
Seasoning
Natural bran to coat

1. Cook onions until tender by stirring in a little yeast extract.

2. Meanwhile add a little of the cold milk to the flour to form a paste and heat the remainder of the milk.

3. Add the hot milk to the blended flour, mix well and add to the onions.

4. Stir the milk over the heat for a few minutes to thicken and then add the cashew nuts, lemon juice and seasoning. Continue to cook for 3 minutes.

5. Leave the mixture to cool on a wet plate.

6. Divide into 8 and coat with bran to form patties.

7. Fry in a non-stick pan or grill to crisp both sides and heat through.

CEREAL AND CHEESE
100gCHO, 720 cals. in total

4 oz (100g) buckwheat/millet (*80gCHO*)
1 tablespoonful fresh parsley, chopped
1 medium onion, finely grated (*5gCHO*)
Seasoning
½ pint (275ml) vegetable stock
1 oz (25g) fresh wholemeal breadcrumbs (*12gCHO*)
2 oz (50g) medium fat cheese, grated
1 egg, beaten
Natural bran to coat

1. Cook the cereal with the onions, herbs and seasoning in the stock until light and fluffy — about 15 minutes.

2. Add the cereal to the remaining ingredients and leave to cool on a wet plate.

3. Divide into 8, coat with bran and bake at 375°F/190°C (Gas Mark 5) for 15 minutes until golden.

SOYA BEAN AND RICE
140gCHO, 1100 cals. in total

6 oz (175g) soya beans soaked overnight (*35gCHO*)
3 oz (75g) brown rice (*65gCHO*)
1 medium onion, finely chopped (*5gCHO*)
2 eggs, beaten
3 oz (75g) fresh wholemeal breadcrumbs (*35gCHO*)
½ teaspoonful celery salt
1 teaspoonful soy sauce
Seasoning

1. Cook beans and rice separately, and drain both.

2. Mash beans and mix with all of the remaining ingredients.

3. Form into patties and bake in a moderate oven 350°F/180°C (Gas Mark 4) until brown or in a 1 lb (450g) loaf tin for about 40 minutes or until firm.

SPINACH AND LENTILS
140gCHO, 900 cals. in total

4 oz (100g) red lentils (*60gCHO*)
1 lb (450g) spinach (*15gCHO*)
6 oz (175g) fresh wholewheat breadcrumbs (*70gCHO*)
1 egg, beaten
1 teaspoonful ground nutmeg
Seasoning
Natural bran to coat

1. Cook lentils until tender and drain off any liquid.

2. Lightly cook spinach, drain and chop finely.

3. Mix all ingredients together, form patties and coat with bran.

4. Fry in a non-stick pan on both sides.

BEAN, RICE AND NUT
140gCHO, 1400 cals. in total

5 oz (150g) cooked brown rice (*50gCHO*)
2 oz (50g) cooked beans, e.g. aduki/kidney (*10gCHO*)
5 oz (150g) hazelnuts, ground (*10gCHO*)
1 teaspoonful dried mixed herbs
2 medium onions, finely chopped (*10gCHO*)
2 medium carrots grated (*10gCHO*)
4 oz (100g) fresh wholemeal breadcrumbs (*50gCHO*)
Seasoning
2 eggs, beaten

1. Mix all the ingredients well, adding the eggs last.

2. Form into rissoles and bake at the top of a moderate oven, 350°F/180°C (Gas Mark 4), for about 30 minutes or until brown.

CARROT, POTATO AND SUNFLOWER
180gCHO, 1500 cals. in total

1½ oz (40g) wholemeal flour (*30gCHO*)
½ pint (275ml) liquid skimmed milk (*15gCHO*)
½ lb (225g) potato, cooked and mashed (*45gCHO*)
1 lb (450g) cooked carrot, mashed (*20gCHO*)
4 oz (100g) sunflower seeds, toasted (*20gCHO*)
4 oz (100g) fresh wholemeal breadcrumbs (*50gCHO*)
2 teaspoonsful ground cumin
2 teaspoonsful dried marjoram
Seasoning
Natural bran to coat

1. Make a paste with the flour and a little of the milk.

2. Heat the rest of the milk and add slowly to the paste.

3. Return the sauce to the heat, stirring until it thickens.

4. Mix the sauce with the remaining ingredients, form into cutlets and bake in a moderate oven, 350°F/180°C (Gas Mark 4), for about 30 minutes or until brown or fry in a non-stick pan.

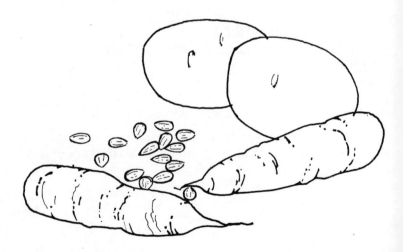

FALAFEL
230gCHO, 1475 cals. in total

1 lb (450g) chick peas, soaked overnight (*225gCHO*)
1 medium onion, grated (*5gCHO*)
6 spring onions, finely chopped
1 tablespoonful lemon juice
2 teaspoonsful ground cumin powder and coriander powder
Bunch fresh parsley, chopped
Chilli pepper
Salt

1. Cook the peas until quite tender and mash.

2. Mix all the ingredients together and leave for 30 minutes.

3. Form into walnut-size balls, flatten slightly and fry in a non-stick pan to brown both sides.

Soufflés

PLAIN SOUFFLÉ
50gCHO, 520 cals. in total

3 large eggs
2 oz (50g) wholemeal flour (*40gCHO*)
½ pint (275ml) liquid skimmed milk (*15gCHO*)
1 teaspoonful made mustard
Herbs
Seasoning

1. Separate the egg yolks and whites.

2. Beat the egg yolks.

3. Make a paste with the flour and a little of the milk.

4. Heat the rest of the milk and then slowly add to the flour paste.

5. Return the sauce to the heat, add mustard, herbs and seasoning, bring to the boil and cook for a few minutes, stirring all the time.

6. Remove from the heat, add the beaten egg yolks and stir well into the mix.

7. Beat the egg whites until stiff and fold into the yolk mixture.

8. Transfer to a soufflé dish and bake at 375°F/190°C (Gas Mark 5) for about 45 minutes.

Variations to basic soufflé
The extras listed below should be added to the white sauce before adding the egg yolks. Add on the CHO and calories of the extras to those of the basic soufflé. Many vegetables can be used as extras — just remember to allow for them.

Extras:	approximate gCHO	cals.
10 oz (275g) asparagus tinned, drained and chopped	negligible	45
6 oz (175g) broccoli/cauliflower, cooked and chopped	negligible	25
6 oz (175g) button mushrooms, sliced	negligible	20
4 oz (100g) cottage cheese, plain	negligible	110
4 oz (100g) cheese medium fat, grated	negligible	345
6 oz (175g) courgettes, cooked	negligible	15
4 oz (100g) leeks, cooked and chopped	negligible	25
6 oz (175g) sweet corn	40	210
2 medium tomatoes, skinned and chopped	negligible	25

Flans

Included here are some very simple low calorie flan bases, together with a selection of fillings. Combine the different bases and fillings to produce a range of dishes, remembering to add their values together. Use non-stick flan tins.

Bases

SIMPLE BREADCRUMB
35gCHO, 190 cals. in total

1. Sprinkle 3 oz (75g) of fresh wholemeal breadcrumbs, mixed with seasonings and herbs, on to the base of a flan tin.

2. Carefully place the filling on top.

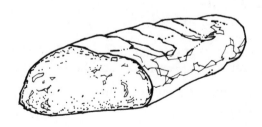

YOGURT AND BREADCRUMB
45gCHO, 260 cals. in total

1. Mix 3 oz (75g) of fresh wholemeal breadcrumbs with a small carton of natural yogurt, herbs and seasoning.

2. Press the paste evenly over the bottom of a flan tin and pour the filling on top.

OAT AND CHEESE
60gCHO, 680 cals. in total

1. Mix 3 oz (75g) of rolled oats with 4 oz (100g) of grated medium fat cheese, seasoning and herbs, and press onto the base of a flan tin.

2. Place filling on top.

CHEESE PASTRY
60gCHO, 530 cals. in total

1. Mix 3 oz (75g) wholemeal flour with 3 oz (75g) medium fat cheese grated, herbs and seasoning.

2. Add sufficient water to form a dough and flatten into a round shape.

3. Press out dough to line a flan tin.

Fillings

BASIC FILLING I
10gCHO, 200 cals. in total

1. Beat together 2 eggs, ¼ pint (150ml) of liquid skimmed milk or natural yogurt, seasoning and herbs.

2. Mix with extras (see later) or pour over extras already placed in the flan case.

3. Bake at 400°F/200°C (Gas Mark 6) for 40 minutes or until set.

4. If liked, the eggs can be separated, and the extras added to the beaten egg yolks before folding in the stiffly beaten egg whites.

5. The following extras can be added to the basic filling:
    —   1 large tin kidney/butter beans, drained; 2 tomatoes skinned and chopped; 2 oz (50g) medium fat cheese, grated (*add on 60gCHO, 530 cals.*);
    —   ½-1 lb (225-450g) free vegetables, chopped, together with a medium onion, chopped (*add on 10gCHO, 50 cals.*).

BASIC FILLING II
10gCHO, 620 cals. in total

1. Slowly mix 1 small carton natural yogurt into ½ lb (225g) curd cheese, followed by 3 beaten eggs, herbs and seasoning.

2. Add any vegetables (see below), pour into the flan case and bake at 350°F/180°C (Gas Mark 4) for 40 minutes or until set.

3. The following extras can be added to the basic filling:
    —   2 medium onions, chopped; 2 spring onions, chopped (*add on 10gCHO, 50 cals.*);
    —   ½ lb (225g) sweetcorn/cooked beans, 1 medium onion, chopped (*add on 40gCHO, 220 cals.*);
    —   1 lb (450g) lightly cooked 'free' vegetables, chopped as necessary; 1 medium onion, chopped (*add on 20gCHO, 140 cals*).

Some More Indian Recipes

Some of these recipes can be used as quickies if the ingredients, such as pulses, are cooked in advance.

PEANUT AND VEGETABLE CURRY
70gCHO, 1400 cals. in total

6 oz (175g) peanuts (*15gCHO*)
4 medium onions, chopped (*20gCHO*)
1 dessertspoonful curry powder
1 teaspoonful garam masala
1 teaspoonful ginger, ground
2 cloves garlic
1 tablespoonful wholemeal flour (*5gCHO*)
1 lb (450g) 'free' vegetables, chopped, e.g. cauliflower, mushrooms, peppers
²/₃ pint (370ml) liquid skimmed milk (*20gCHO*)
Seasoning

1. Soak and cook the peanuts (1 hour soaking, then 30 minutes in a pressure cooker or overnight soaking and 2-3 hours cooking).

2. Gently cook the onions, curry powder, garam masala, ginger and garlic in a non-stick pan until the onions are tender.

3. Make a paste with the flour and a little of the milk.

4. Heat the rest of the milk and slowly add to the paste, mixing well.

5. Pour the milk and flour mix over the onions, add peanuts and seasoning and cook for about 15-20 minutes, stirring occasionally and adding the vegetables towards the end.

6. Serve garnished with slices of raw tomato or cucumber.

BEAN CURRY

100gCHO, 560 cals. in total

1 lb (450g) fresh tomatoes, skinned and chopped, or 1 large tin (*10gCHO*)
2 medium onions, chopped (*10gCHO*)
2 medium carrots, diced (*10gCHO*)
2 teaspoonsful cumin seeds
½ teaspoonful chilli powder
Seasoning
1 lb (450g) cooked kidney beans/chick peas/split peas (*70gCHO*)

1. In a large pan cook all the ingredients apart from the beans, until the carrots are quite tender.

2. Add the cooked beans and cook for about 10 minutes to blend the flavours.

Note: If soya beans are used in this recipe then the dish will contain *70gCHO, 720 cals*.

PEA AND POTATO PATTIES (Matar alu tikki)
110gCHO, 620 cals. in total

1 lb (450g) cooked and mashed potatoes (*90gCHO*)
1 oz (25g) wholemeal flour (*12gCHO*)
4 oz (100g) fresh/frozen peas (*5gCHO*)
1 tablespoonful desiccated coconut
2 tablespoonsful fresh coriander leaves/parsley, chopped
½ teaspoonful turmeric powder
½ teaspoonful paprika/chilli powder
Juice half lemon
Seasoning

1. Knead the flour into the potatoes.

2. Mix the peas with the rest of the ingredients and mash well.

3. Divide the potato into walnut-size balls, flatten and place a little of the pea mixture on each.

4. Shape the potato into small balls to enclose the filling and then flatten again.

5. Fry in a non-stick pan on both sides to cook thoroughly and brown.

SPINACH AND LENTILS (Dal sag)
140gCHO, 820 cals. in total

½ lb (225g) mixed lentils (*120gCHO*)
1 lb (450g) spinach, finely chopped (*15gCHO*)
1 medium onion, chopped (*5gCHO*)
1 teaspoonful mustard powder
½ teaspoonful turmeric powder
½ teaspoonful paprika/chilli powder
½ teaspoonful cumin powder
1 teaspoonful sea salt
1 teaspoonful garam masala

1. Wash the lentils and leave to soak.

2. Boil 3 cupsful of water, add the drained lentils, onion and spices (except garam masala) and cook for 5 minutes.

3. Add spinach to the lentils and keep on a medium heat until the lentils are cooked, adding a little more water if necessary to prevent the dish from drying.

4. Mix in the garam masala towards the end of the cooking time. (1 large tin of tomatoes can be substituted for the spinach.)

VEGETABLE PULAU (Sabzi pulau)
200gCHO, 1080 cals. in total

1 in. (2cm) piece fresh ginger
2 green chillis, chopped (optional)
2 bay leaves
1 tablespoonful fresh coriander leaves or parsley, chopped
½ teaspoonful turmeric powder
½ lb (225g) brown rice (*175gCHO*)
1 teaspoonful garam masala
Sea salt
1 large onion, finely chopped (*10gCHO*)
½ lb (225g) fresh/frozen peas (*10gCHO*)
½ lb (225g) green beans
2 large tomatoes, skinned and chopped (*5gCHO*)

1. Grind ginger, chillis, bay leaves, coriander and turmeric together.

2. Bring ¾ pint (425ml) water to the boil, add rice, ginger paste, garam masala and salt, and bring to the boil again.

3. Cover the rice and simmer undisturbed until cooked and the water is absorbed.

4. Meanwhile cook the vegetables together and stir into the rice just before serving.

RICE AND LENTILS (Khichhari)
250gCHO, 1320 cals. in total

This dish must be carefully cooked so that it does not become mushy. Split peas can be substituted for the lentils and additional vegetables can be incorporated into the final dish provided that any extra carbohydrate and calories are added on.

1 tablespoonful fresh coriander leaves/parsley, chopped
1 in. (2cm) piece fresh ginger
4 cloves garlic
½ teaspoonful turmeric powder
½ teaspoonful paprika/chilli powder
½ teaspoonful garam masala
6 oz (175g) long grain brown rice (*130gCHO*)
6 oz (175g) green lentils/peas (*90gCHO*)
1 medium onion, chopped (*5gCHO*)
2 green chillis, finely chopped
2 large tomatoes, skinned and quartered (*5gCHO*)
4 oz (100g) potatoes, diced (*20gCHO*)
½ teaspoonful cumin seeds/powder
Seasoning

1. Pound the coriander, ginger, garlic, turmeric powder, paprika and garam masala together in a mortar.

2. Place rice, lentils, onions, ginger paste and cumin, chillis and seasoning in a saucepan with 1 ¼ pints (700ml) water and bring to the boil.

3. Lower the heat and leave to simmer for about 15 minutes.

4. Add the tomatoes and potato to the rice and continue to simmer for another 20-25 minutes until the rice and lentils are cooked.

Desserts

Recipe	gCHO	calories	page
Baked Apples/Pears with Soft Fruit	50	200	154
Lemon and Pineapple Bake	50	260	154
Swiss Roll, plain (filling extra)	50	600	154
Baked Bananas	70	380	155
Apple Pudding	70	700	156
Brandied Apricots	80	800	156
Fruit Cheesecake	90	1170	157
Summer Pudding	100	470	158
Semolina Cream with Peach Purée	100	640	158
Baked Apples/Pears with Fruit and Nuts	120	600	159
No-cook Cheesecake	120	1680	159
Baked Flaked Rice Pudding	140	880	160
Apricot Pizza	150	850	160
Cooked Fruit Pudding	150	1000	161
Frozen Desserts			162
Raspberry Water Ice	10	180	162
Berry Sorbet	15	300	162
Orange Water Ice	40	180	162
Strawberry and Yogurt Freeze	40	220	163
Peach Mousse	40	380	164
Ice Cream I	20	280	164
Ice Cream II	30	520	164
Ice Cream III	30	640	165

Some ideas for ways with fruit, as well as toppings for dishes can be found on pages 23 to 51. Here are some more suggestions for when you have some time to spare, again often centred around fruit as the most important ingredient. If a recipe has a number of eggs in it, use this dish to follow a main course such as a vegetable curry or a hot pot.

BAKED APPLES/PEARS WITH SOFT FRUIT
50gCHO, 200 cals. in total

4 apples/pears (*40gCHO*)
6 oz (175g) soft fruit (raspberries, blackcurrants) (*10gCHO*)

1. Wash and core the apples or pears.

2. Pile the soft fruit into the scooped-out cores of the apple or pears.

3. Wrap in foil and place in a dish and bake at 375°F/190°C (Gas Mark 5) for 30-40 minutes.

EASY LEMON AND PINEAPPLE BAKE
50gCHO, 260 cals. in total

1 oz (25g) fresh wholemeal breadcrumbs (*12gCHO*)
½ lb (225g) tin crushed pineapple in natural juice (*35gCHO*)
½ lemon
1 egg, beaten

1. Place the breadcrumbs in a bowl, add the pineapple and its juice, grated rind of the lemon and its juice and the beaten egg.

2. Beat well and turn the mixture into 1 pint (550ml) shallow dish and cook for 15-20 minutes at 425°F/220°C (Gas Mark 7).

SWISS ROLL
50gCHO, 600 cals. — without filling

This basic sponge roll can be filled with just fruit or a mixture of fruit and curd cheese.

3 eggs, separated
1½ oz (40g) fructose
2½ oz (65g) wholemeal flour (*50gCHO*)

1. Whisk the egg whites until stiff, then add the beaten egg yolks and whisk until blended into the whites.

2. Add the fructose and whisk further until the mixture is thick and creamy.

3. With a metal spoon, lightly fold in the flour with 1 tablespoonful warm water until evenly blended.

4. Pour on to a non-stick Swiss roll tin and tilt to spread evenly.

5. Bake at 425°F/220°C (Gas Mark 7) for 7-10 minutes when it should be just springy.

6. Turn out on to a dampened greaseproof paper, spread with filling (see below) and roll up.

7. Leave to cool on a wire rack.

Fruit Purée Filling
30gCHO, 180 cals. in total

Cook 12 oz (350g) soft fruit (blackcurrants, blackberries), 1 chopped apple and ½ oz (15g) fructose together, until fruit is tender.

If you are also using curd cheese as a spread, wait for the sponge to cool. Add on 40 calories for every 1 oz (25g) of cheese used.

BAKED BANANAS
70gCHO, 380 cals. in total

6 small bananas (*60gCHO*)
Juice 2 oranges (*10gCHO*)
1 tablespoonful rum
1 tablespoonful dessicated coconut, toasted

1. Split the bananas in half and place in a shallow dish.

2. Mix the orange juice and rum and pour over.

3. Bake at 300°F/150°C (Gas Mark 2) for about 20 minutes basting occasionally.

4. Serve sprinkled with the toasted coconut.

APPLE PUDDING
70gCHO, 700 cals. in total

1 lb apples (*40gCHO*)
3 eggs, separated
1 oz (25g) fructose
1½ oz (40g) wholemeal flour (*30gCHO*)
1 tablespoonful ground almonds
Grated rind and juice 1 lemon
½ teaspoonful cinnamon

1. Peel and core apples and grate.

2. Whisk the egg whites until stiff.

3. Beat the yolks with the fructose and then stir in all of the remaining items except for the egg whites, which should be folded in last.

4. Bake at 375°F/190°C (Gas Mark 5) for 1 hour. Serve hot or cold.

Note: Firm pears can be substituted for the apples.

BRANDIED APRICOTS
80gCHO, 800 cals. in total

1 lemon
16 medium apricots (*50gCHO*)
8 tablespoonsful apricot brandy (*30gCHO*)
5 oz (150g) plain cottage cheese
2 oz (50g) curd cheese
1 oz (25g) hazelnuts, chopped and toasted

1. Grate the lemon rind and strain the juice of the lemon.

2. Gently poach the apricots with the brandy, 1 tablespoonful lemon juice and ¼ pint (150ml) water until the apricots are just tender.

3. Remove the apricots from the liquid and cool, meanwhile boil the poaching liquid for another 3-4 minutes to reduce and leave to cool.

4. Skin the apricots and slice in half.

5. Beat together the cheeses or blend in a liquidizer, until smooth and add a little of the poaching liquid together with the lemon rind.

6. Sandwich each of the apricot halves together with the cheese mixture, place in a bowl and spoon the poaching liquid over.

7. Decorate with the hazelnuts.

FRUIT CHEESECAKE
90gCHO, 1170 cals. in total

2 large oranges (*20gCHO*)
6 wholemeal biscuits (*60gCHO*)
Grated rind 1 lemon
12 oz (350g) curd cheese
2 eggs, beaten
1 tablespoonful concentrated natural unsweetened orange juice
  (*10gCHO*)

1. Grate the rind of the oranges.

2. Crumble the biscuits and sprinkle over the base of a non-stick flan tin, ideally loose-bottomed.

3. Blend together the orange and lemon rind, cheese, eggs and fruit juice and pour the mixture carefully onto the crumb base.

4. Bake for 45 minutes at 350°F/180°C (Gas Mark 4), then cool and remove from tin.

5. Decorate with slices of fresh orange.

Note: The same weight of fruit such as pears, peaches, apples can be used and the value of the dish will be the same.

SUMMER PUDDING
100gCHO, 470 cals. in total

1 oz (25g) concentrated unsweetened orange juice (*20gCHO*)
1 lb (450g) soft fruit (blackberries, blackcurrants) (*30gCHO*)
4 oz (100g) crustless wholemeal bread slices (*50gCHO*)

1. Place the juice and 2 tablespoonsful water in a saucepan, heat gently and add the fruit.

2. Cook the fruit until just tender and remove from the heat, allowing to cool.

3. Cut the bread into fingers and line the sides and base of a 1 pint (550ml) basin, reserving sufficient bread for the top.

4. Pour in the fruit mixture and cover with the remaining bread, put a saucer and weight on top and leave in a cool place for 4-5 hours.

SEMOLINA CREAM WITH PEACH PURÉE
100gCHO, 640 cals. in total

1½ oz (40g) wholewheat semolina (*30gCHO*)
⅔ pint (370ml) liquid skimmed milk (*20gCHO*)
2 eggs, separated
1 large tin (15 oz/425g) peaches in natural juice (*45gCHO*)

1. Sprinkle the semolina over the milk in a pan and bring to the boil.

2. Simmer for 2-3 minutes, stirring and remove from the heat.

3. Beat in the egg yolks.

4. Purée the fruit and juice together and stir half into the semolina.

5. Stiffly whisk the egg whites and fold into the mixture.

6. Spoon into a 2½ pints (1.4 litres) dish and bake at 375°F/190°C (Gas Mark 5) for about 40 minutes.

7. Serve with the rest of the fruit purée, warmed.

BAKED APPLES/PEARS WITH FRUIT AND NUTS
120gCHO, 600 cals. in total

4 apples/pears (*40gCHO*)
4 oz (100g) stoned dates (*80gCHO*)
1 oz (25g) walnuts, chopped
Juice ½ lemon

1. Wash and core the apples or pears.

2. Chop the dates and mix with the fruit and nuts.

3. Pile into the hollows of the apples or pears, wrap in foil and place in a dish.

4. Bake at 375°F/190°C (Gas Mark 5) for 30-40 minutes.

NO-COOK CHEESECAKE
120gCHO, 1680 cals. in total

3 oz (75g) muesli biscuits (*60gCHO*)
1½ lb (675g) curd cheese
Rind 1 orange, grated
3 fl oz (75ml) unsweetened concentrated natural fruit juice (*60gCHO*)

1. Crumble the biscuits and sprinkle on the base of a non-stick flan tin (ideally loose-bottomed).

2. Beat together the cheese, orange rind and juice until smooth.

3. Pour or spoon the mixture carefully onto the biscuit base, cover and chill.

BAKED FLAKED RICE PUDDING
140gCHO, 880 cals. in total

3 oz (75g) brown rice flakes (*65gCHO*)
2 oz (50g) raisins/sultanas (*35gCHO*)
1⅓ pints (735ml) liquid skimmed milk (*40gCHO*)
½ oz (15g) desiccated coconut
1 oz (25g) low fat spread
Grated nutmeg

1. Place rice, raisins, milk and coconut into a 2 pint (1 litre) dish and leave for 1 hour, then stir.

2. Float flakes of low fat spread over the top, sprinkle with nutmeg and bake at 350°F/180°C (Gas Mark 4) for about 1 hour or until the pudding is rising in large bubbles.

3. Lower the heat to 275°F/140°C (Gas Mark 1) and continue cooking for another ½ hour.

APRICOT PIZZA
150gCHO, 850 cals. in total

½ oz (15g) fresh yeast
1 egg
1 oz (25g) fructose
6 oz (175g) wholemeal flour (*115gCHO*)
10 oz (275g) tin apricots in natural juice (*35gCHO*)
1 heaped teaspoonful cinnamon

1. Blend the yeast with 2 tablespoonsful of warm water.

2. Place the egg and half the fructose in a mixing bowl and beat together.

3. Beat the yeast liquid into the egg and finally add the flour to form a soft dough, kneading until smooth.

4. Cover and leave for about 40 minutes in a warm place until the dough has nearly doubled in size.

5. Heat a non-stick frying pan until warm to the touch but not hot and remove from the heat.

6. Knead the dough for another minute, place in the warmed pan and press out to fill the base.

7. Drain the apricots and arrange the halves in rings over the dough.

8. Mix the remaining fructose with the cinnamon and sprinkle over the apricots. Cover and again leave in a warm place for 20 minutes to rise.

9. Place the pan on a low heat, cook gently for 15-20 minutes until the dough is risen and firm and the underside golden.

10. Meanwhile simmer the fruit juice to reduce and thicken.

11. Remove the pizza carefully from the pan onto a warm serving plate and serve with the hot juice.

Variation: Peaches can be used instead of apricots.

COOKED FRUIT PUDDING
150gCHO, 1000 cals. in total

½ lb (225g) fresh wholemeal breadcrumbs (*100gCHO*)
½ pint (275ml) liquid skimmed milk (*15gCHO*)
½ lb (225g) soft fruit (blackberries, blackcurrants) (*15gCHO*)
1 oz (25g) unsweetened concentrated natural orange/apple juice
  (*20gCHO*)
½ teaspoonful cinnamon
1 egg, beaten
1 oz (25g) nuts, chopped

1. Pour the milk over the breadcrumbs and soak for ¾ hour.

2. Mix the fruit, juice, spice and beaten egg together and then stir in the softened breadcrumbs.

3. Top with the nuts and bake at 350°F/180°C (Gas Mark 4) for 1½-2 hours.

Frozen Desserts

Set the freezer to maximum for these recipes.

RASPBERRY WATER ICE
10gCHO, 180 cals. in total

6 oz (175g) raspberries (*10gCHO*)
1 oz (25g) fructose
2 teaspoonsful lemon juice
2 egg whites, stiffly beaten

1. Mash or purée the berries and mix well with the fructose and lemon juice.

2. Freeze until half frozen and mushy and fold in the beaten egg whites.

3. Re-freeze covered with foil until firm.

BERRY SORBET
15gCHO, 300 cals. in total

½ lb (225g) blackcurrants/blackberries (*15gCHO*)
1 oz (25g) fructose
2 teaspoonsful lemon juice

1. Purée the fruit.

2. Dissolve the fructose in a little hot water and make up to ¾ pint (425ml).

3. Mix the fruit and water together, cover with foil and freeze until starting to set.

4. Whisk well to trap the air, return to the freezer and repeat this one or two more times.

Variation: Raspberries or strawberries can be used in this recipe.

ORANGE WATER ICE
40gCHO, 180 cals. in total

4 large oranges (*40gCHO*)
Juice ½ lemon
2 egg whites, stiffly beaten

1. Liquidize the flesh of the oranges and mix with 1 tablespoonful finely grated rind from one of the oranges, and the lemon juice.

2. Add ½ pint (275ml) water and mix well.

3. Freeze until the mixture begins to set, beat thoroughly and fold in the stiffly beaten egg whites.

4. Re-freeze until just soft enough to scoop out.

STRAWBERRY AND YOGURT FREEZE
40gCHO, 220 cals. in total

12 oz (350g) strawberries (*20gCHO*)
2 small cartons natural yogurt (*20gCHO*)

1. Freeze the yogurt until mushy and add the mashed strawberries.

2. Freeze again until starting to set, beat until smooth and freeze again.

3. This dessert becomes very hard, so transfer to an ordinary fridge about two hours before required.

Variation: Raspberries can be used instead of strawberries but you may need to add ½ oz/15g fructose — *50 cals.*

PEACH MOUSSE
40gCHO, 380 cals. in total

4 large peaches (*40gCHO*)
1 oz (25g) coconut cream, grated

1. Skin and stone the peaches, chop and purée in a blender.

2. Add the coconut cream.

3. Freeze for 2 hours, removing 15 minutes before serving.

ICE CREAM I
20gCHO, 280 cals. in total

2 small cartons natural yogurt (*20gCHO*)
1 oz (25g) fructose
Few drops vanilla essence
2 egg whites

1. Beat together the yogurt, fructose and vanilla essence.

2. Partly freeze, turn into a large bowl, add any extras and fold in the stiffly beaten egg whites.

3. Freeze again.

ICE CREAM II
30gCHO, 520 cals. in total

1 small carton natural yogurt (*10gCHO*)
½ lb (225g) plain cottage cheese, liquidized or sieved
⅔ pint (370ml) liquid skimmed milk (*20gCHO*)
1 oz (25g) fructose
Few drops vanilla essence

1. Blend all ingredients well.

2. Freeze, removing from time to time to whip air in.

3. Remove from the freezer about 1 hour before it is required for the meal.

ICE CREAM III
30gCHO, 640 cals. in total

1 large carton natural yogurt (*30gCHO*)
12 oz (350g) plain cottage cheese, liquidized or sieved
1 oz (25g) fructose
Few drops vanilla essence

Follow method for Ice Cream II.

Note: If curd cheese, instead of cottage is used in the previous two recipes then No. II will contain *600 cals.* and No. III, *760 cals.*

Extras for ice cream
To any of the ice creams you can add one or more of the following, but remember to add on the extra carbohydrate and calories.

	gCHO	cals.
4 oz (100g) apricots dried, soaked and puréed	50	200
2 small bananas, mashed	20	90
2 tablespoonsful brandy/rum/whisky	negligible	65
1 tablespoonful instant coffee, dissolved in 1 tablespoonful hot water	negligible	negligible
1 oz (25g) currants/dates/raisins/sultanas	20	70
Few drops essence e.g. almond, pistachio, (omit vanilla in recipe)	negligible	negligible
3 tablespoonsful 100% fruit jam/marmalade	20	80
Juice and grated rind 1 large grapefruit	10	40
2 oz (50g) nuts chopped and roasted	negligible	320
Juice and grated rind 2 oranges	10	40
2 tablespoonsful orange flower/rosewater	negligible	negligible
6 oz (175g) soft fruit — strawberries/raspberries	10	40

7.

Goodies

NUT CAKE
20gCHO, 1060 cals., using hazelnuts
20gCHO, 1260 cals., using walnuts
20gCHO, 1300 cals., using almonds

3 eggs, separated
2 oz (50g) fructose
1 tablespoonful rum/whisky/dry sherry
5 oz (150g) ground nuts (*CHO variable*)
1 oz (25g) fresh wholemeal breadcrumbs (*12gCHO*)

1. Whisk egg yolks with fructose until thick and creamy.

2. Beat egg whites until stiff but not dry.

3. Fold the whites into the yolks, alternately with the nuts and bread crumbs.

4. Pour into a non-stick 7-8 in. (12-15cm) cake tin and bake for 40-45 minutes at 350°F/180°C (Gas Mark 4).

5. You can cut and then sandwich this cake with curd cheese and/or chopped roasted nuts and/or sliced or puréed fruit. It can also be decorated with fruit or nuts and glazed with melted 100 per cent fruit jam. Do remember, however to add on the extra carbohydrate and calories.

SPICY CARROT CAKE
30gCHO, 1340 cals. in total

Ingredients for Nut Cake (using almonds), as above (*20gCHO*)
2 medium carrots, minced (*10gCHO*)
Grated rind 1 orange
1 teaspoonful mixed spice/cinnamon

Follow the method for Nut Cake but mix in carrots, rind and spice before adding the egg whites.

CHAROSETH

60gCHO, 680 cals. in total

½ lb (225g) eating apples (*20gCHO*)
2 oz (50g) raisins, chopped (*40gCHO*)
2 oz (50g) nuts, chopped
Lemon juice
Ground cinnamon
1 oz (25g) ground nuts

1. Peel and core the apples and chop finely.

2. Mix apples with raisins and nuts.

3. Add a little lemon juice and cinnamon to taste.

4. Mix well and form into small balls. Coat with ground nuts.

CREAMY SESAME AND DATE BALLS

60gCHO, 1260 cals. in total

½ lb (225g) curd cheese
4 oz (100g) sesame seeds, roasted and ground (*20gCHO*)
2 oz (50g) dates, finely chopped (*35gCHO*)
Lemon juice
1 oz (25g) sesame seeds, roasted (*5gCHO*)

1. Mix all the ingredients well except for the whole sesame seeds.

2. Form into small firm balls and coat with sesame seeds.

3. Leave in the fridge overnight to harden.

SIMPLE SPONGE
75gCHO, 830 cals. in total

4 eggs, separated
2 oz (50g) fructose
Few drops vanilla essence
4 oz (100g) wholemeal flour (*75gCHO*)
1 heaped teaspoonful baking powder

1. Whisk egg yolks with the fructose until they are thick, creamy and light.

2. Whisk in the vanilla essence.

3. Sift the flour and baking powder and add back the bran.

4. Beat the egg whites until stiff but not dry and fold in alternately with the flour to the yolks.

5. Bake in a 9 in. (23cm) non-stick cake tin for about 1 hour at 325°F/170°C (Gas Mark 3) or until springy.

6. You can add the fillings and toppings suggested for the Nut Cake (page 167).

MACAROONS
85gCHO, 1520 cals. in total

2 eggs, separated
2 oz (50g) fructose
Grated rind 1 orange/lemon
Few drops vanilla essence
4 oz (100g) desiccated coconut (*5gCHO*)
4 oz (100g) whole wheat breakfast flakes (*80gCHO*)

1. Beat the egg yolks with the fructose until thick creamy and light.

2. Whisk in rind and essence.

3. Crumble wheat flakes mix with the coconut, and fold into the yolks alternately with stiffly beaten egg whites.

4. Drop from a teaspoonful on to a non-stick baking tray and cook for about 12 minutes at 375°F/190°C (Gas Mark 5) or until slightly brown.

YOGURT DROP SCONES
100gCHO, 700 cals. in total

2 eggs, separated
½ oz (15g) fructose
2 small cartons natural yogurt (*20gCHO*)
4 oz (100g) wholemeal flour (*75gCHO*)
Rind 1 orange, grated
1 teaspoonful mixed spice/ground cinnamon

1. Beat egg yolks and fructose until light, thick and creamy.

2. Beat in the yogurt.

3. Beat the egg whites until stiff but not dry.

4. Fold the flour mixed with the spice and rind, alternately into the egg yolks with the beaten egg whites.

5. Drop spoonsful on to a large non-stick frying pan and cook until bubbles start to appear.

6. Turn to cook the other side.

7. Serve hot with fruit purée or 100 per cent fruit jam melted together with curd cheese or yogurt. Add on the carbohydrate and calories of any extras.

FRUIT AND NUT SLICES
165gCHO, 1180 cals. in total

10 oz (275g) dried apples/apricots (*120gCHO*)
2 oz (50g) raisins/sultanas/dates (*40gCHO*)
4 oz (100g) nuts, ground (*5gCHO*)
Lemon juice
1 teaspoonful mixed spice/cinnamon/ginger

1. Wash the fruit but leave the moisture clinging to it.

2. Chop the fruit finely and mix with other ingredients, adding enough lemon juice to bind the fruit.

3. Press into a 7 in. (18cm) shallow tin, ideally lined with rice paper, and cover either with rice paper or greaseproof.

4. Leave in the fridge overnight to harden and cut with a knife just dipped in hot water.

CORNBREAD
200gCHO, 2000 cals. in total

1 egg, beaten
½ oz (15g) fructose
1 teaspoonful lemon juice
⅓ pint (185ml) liquid skimmed milk (*10gCHO*)
6 oz (175g) corn (maize) meal (*115gCHO*)
4 oz (100g) wholemeal flour (*75gCHO*)
1 tablespoonful baking powder
½ teaspoonful sea salt

1. Whisk eggs with the fructose, lemon juice and milk.

2. Sift the dry ingredients and add back the bran from the flour.

3. Hollow out the centre of the dry ingredients and stir in the egg mixture.

4. Spoon the batter into a bun tin and bake at 425°F/220°C (Gas Mark 7) for 10-12 minutes, or into a 8 in. (20cm) square cake tin and bake for 20-25 minutes.

5. Serve hot with a savoury dish, e.g. a vegetable casserole or spead them with 100 per cent fruit jam and have them as a snack.

6. This mix can also be used as a topping for a vegetable base (page 30).

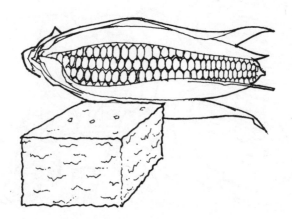

BRAN MUFFINS

240gCHO, 1340 cals. in total

10 oz (275g) wholemeal flour (*190gCHO*)
1 teaspoonful baking powder
4 oz (100g) bran (*20gCHO*)
2 oz (50g) fructose
½ teaspoonful ground cinnamon
Pinch ground cloves
Pinch nutmeg
1 pint (550ml) liquid skimmed milk (*30gCHO*)
Few drops vanilla essence
2 egg whites

1. Sift flour and baking powder and add back the bran.

2. Mix together all the dry ingredients.

3. Combine the milk and vanilla essence and add to the dry ingredients.

4. Beat the egg whites until stiff but not dry and fold into the bran mixture.

5. Spoon into a bun tin and bake at 400°F/200°C (Gas Mark 6) for 20 minutes.

FRUITY FIBRE LOAF
280gCHO, 1280 cals. in total

4 oz (100g) All Bran (*50gCHO*)
6 oz (175g) dried apricots (*75gCHO*)
4 oz (100g) raisins/sultanas (*70gCHO*)
Grated rind 1 lemon
1 eating apple (*10gCHO*)
½ pint (275ml) cold tea
1 teaspoonful mixed spice
4 oz (100g) self-raising wholemeal flour (*75gCHO*)

1. Soak All Bran, fruit (chopped as necessary), lemon rind in the tea for ½ hour.

2. Sieve in the flour, adding back the bran, and the spice and mix well.

3. Bake in a 2 lb (1 kilo) loaf tin at 350°F/180°C (Gas Mark 4) for 50-60 minutes.

4. Turn out of tin and leave to cool.

8.

Worth a Try

Tips in General

Develop a different attitude to food — what you eat should be good for you rather than harming you in any way, either from the quantity or quality point of view.

Keep to the unrefined foods — they are bulkier and you will feel less hungry.

Get to know which foods to avoid.

Wherever possible, carry your own snacks with you — then you will not need to buy unsuitable foods when out.

Wherever possible take lunch with you, especially if you are uncertain of the type of food, if any, which will be available.

Do not skip snacks or meals (particularly if you are diabetic).

Eat slowly and do not eat whilst reading/working etc. Be aware of what you have eaten.

Do not get desperate and binge on unsuitable foods — remember how miserable and unwell you will feel afterwards.

Try to lose your sweet tooth by not relying on sweeteners, artificial or otherwise.

Exercise is very important — it increases your metabolism during and following the exercise period. It helps to use up the energy (calories) in the food you have eaten and it makes you feel better.

Tips for the Weight-watcher

It is important to think about why you need to lose weight — a compulsive eater may be looking to food for comfort because of emotional problems. You must convince yourself that overeating fails to help in any way. Shedding those unnecessary pounds is good for your health and will help you to feel happier about your appearance.

Do not nibble unconsciously, for example when cooking or watching T.V. Be aware of how much you are consuming, having decided what your intake for the day should be.

Do not weigh yourself daily — there are often fluctuations during the day and from day to day. Once a week at the same time is quite sufficient.

Try to keep a check on your weight for yourself. However if you are really lacking will-power — make a promise to persevere to someone close to you and keep to it!

Record your weight loss on a graph. The following graph plan (page 177) will help you.

Have low calorie or calorie free snacks available e.g. celery, cucumber, carrot.

Tips for the Diabetic

The quality of the carbohydrate eaten is very important. The fibre in the unrefined cereals, pulses, fruit and vegetables etc. helps to prevent the blood sugar swings which you can get when eating refined sugars and starches. Fibre is also thought to prevent the build up of unnecessary fats in the blood.

Whole fruit is better than fruit juice which is concentrated and has had the fibre of the fruit removed.

Fats and oils — too much is thought to reduce the effective-

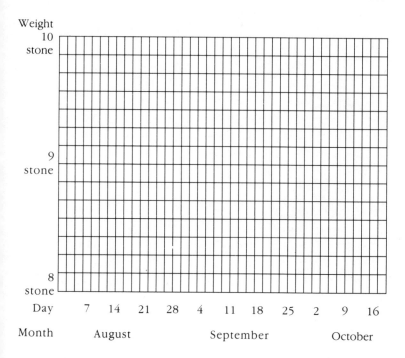

ness of insulin either directly or indirectly. Nuts and seeds, although they have a considerable fat content, do not seem to have the same extreme effect, possibly because of their nature or because of the fibre present in the seeds.

Aim to get your protein from the less concentrated plant foods which are also high in fibre, rather than the fibreless animal protein foods.

Muesli (see page 115) has a very good combination of ingredients — some are more easily digested than others and this is particularly useful for a bedtime snack for diabetics to last them through the night.

Exercise is very important, particularly on a regular basis. If, as a diabetic, there is a certain time during the day when the blood sugar tends to rise, exercise at this time may help.

Appendix

Food	Amount	CHO (approx.)	Calories (approx.)
almonds, shelled	1 oz/25g	neg	140
apples,			
cooking, fresh, whole	1 lb/450g	35	140
eating, fresh, whole	1 lb/450g	40	160
apple juice, unsweetened	¼ pt/150ml	18	70
apple juice, concentrated			
unsweetened	1 fl oz/25ml	20	85
apricots, dried	1 oz/25g	11	45
fresh, whole	1 lb/450g	28	125
canned in natural juice	10 oz/284g can	35	135
artichokes, globe, whole,			
raw	1 lb/450g	20	130
jerusalem, whole, raw	1 lb/450g	50	200 max
aubergine, fresh, whole, raw	1 lb/450g	11	50
asparagus, fresh, raw	1 lb/450g	12	60
avocado pear, fresh, whole,			
1 average	8 oz/225g	3	360
bamboo shoots, canned	1x10 oz/285g can	12	80
banana, peeled	2 oz/50g	10	40
barley, pot raw	1 oz/25g	18	85
beans,			
broad, fresh/frozen	1 oz/25g	2	15
butter, canned	1x15 oz/425g can	50	280
dried	1 oz/25g	12	70
haricot, canned	1x15 oz/425g can	40	280
dried	1 oz/25g	12	70

Food	Amount	CHO (approx.)	Calories (approx.)
mung, dried	1 oz/25g	9	60
pinto, dried	1 oz/25g	15	70
runner, fresh/frozen	1 oz/25g	neg	5
soya, canned	1x15 oz/425g can	22	500
dried	1 oz/25g	7	100
bean shoots/sprouts	1 lb/450g	10	50
beetroot, fresh, cooked	1 lb/450g	35	160
blackberries, fresh/frozen	1 lb/450g	30	120
blackcurrants, fresh/frozen	1 lb/450g	30	120
bran, natural	1 oz/25g	5	30
Brazil nuts	1 oz/25g	neg	160
bread, wholemeal	1 oz/25g	10	60
broccoli, fresh, raw, whole	1 lb/450g	10	70
Brussel sprouts, fresh, raw, whole	1 lb/450g	9	80
buckwheat, raw	1 oz/25g	19	85
cabbage, fresh, raw	1 lb/450g	15	100
carob powder	1 oz/25g	20	45
carrots, fresh, raw	1 lb/450g	20	100
cashew nuts	1 oz/25g	7	140
cauliflower, fresh, raw	1 lb/450g	5	40
celeriac, fresh, raw	1 lb/450g	30	100
celery, fresh, raw	1 head	neg	30
cereal flakes, mixed (muesli base)	1 oz/25g	16	80-100
cheese, cottage	1 oz/25g	neg	25
curd	1 oz/25g	neg	40
Edam	1 oz/25g	neg	75
Gouda	1 oz/25g	neg	75
quark	1 oz/25g	neg	25
cherries, fresh, whole	1 lb/450g	40	160
chestnuts, dried	1 oz/25g	22	105
skinned, fresh, raw	1 oz/25g	10	45
chick peas, canned	1x15 oz/425g can	60	280
dried	1 oz/25g	12	80
chicory, fresh, raw	1 lb/450g	10	60
coconut, cream	1 oz/25g	neg	160
desiccated	1 oz/25g	neg	150
fresh	1 oz/25g	neg	90
corn (maize) meal	1 oz/25g	18	90
corn on cob, whole, raw	1 lb/450g	70	380

Food	Amount	CHO (approx.)	Calories (approx.)
courgette, fresh, raw, whole	1 lb/450g	15	100
cranberries, fresh, raw	1 lb/450g	15	70
cucumber, fresh	1 large	neg	30
currants, dried	1 oz/25g	16	60
damsons, fresh, whole, raw	1 lb/450g	40	150
dates, dried, pitted	2 small	10	40
fresh, whole	2 medium	10	40
egg, 1 whole	size 3	neg	80
1 white	size 3	neg	10
1 yolk	size 3	neg	70
endive, fresh, raw (see chicory)			
figs, dried	1	10	40
fresh	1	10	40
flour, wholemeal	1 lb/450g	300	1440
soya, low fat	1 lb/450g	120	1590
full fat	1 lb/450g	90	1940
brown rice	1 lb/450g	350	1620
fructose	1 oz/25g	*see note	100
fruit salad, canned in natural juice	1x10 oz/285g can	35	135
garlic	1 clove	neg	neg
gooseberries, fresh, whole, raw	1 lb/450g	15	75
grapefruit, canned in natural juice	1x10 oz/285g can	30	120
fresh	1 medium	5	20
grapefruit, juice, unsweetened	¼ pint/150ml	13	60
grapes, fresh, whole	10 large	10	40
grape juice, unsweetened	¼ pint/150ml	22	90
greengages, fresh	1 lb/450g	50	200
hazel nuts, shelled	1 oz/25g	neg	100
honey	1 oz/25g	20	75
kiwi fruit	2 average	10	40
ladies fingers (okra), fresh, raw	1 lb/450g	9	70
macaroni, wholewheat, raw	8 oz/225g	150	720
malt extract	1 oz/25g	23	105

*Approx 30g CHO per ounce but usually ignored by diabetics providing not more than 1 ounce is taken in any one day as part of a recipe.

Food	Amount	CHO (approx.)	Calories (approx.)
mandarins, canned in natural juice	1x10 oz/285g can	15-20	80
fresh	2 average	10	40
mango, fresh	1 large	30	120
margarine, low fat	1 oz/25g	*neg*	95
vegetable	1 oz/25g	*neg*	200
marrow, fresh, raw, whole	1 lb/450g	8	40
melon, fresh, honeydew, whole	1 lb/450g	13	55
water, whole	1 lb/450g	12	50
milk, skimmed, fresh	1 pint/550ml	27-30	180
skimmed, dried powder	1 oz/25g	14	90
millet	1 oz/25g	18	95
miso	1 tblsp/15mlsp	*neg*	10
mixed vegetables, frozen	1 oz/25g	3	20
mushrooms, fresh, raw	1 lb/450g	*neg*	70
nectarines, fresh, whole	1 lb/450g	50	200
nuts, mixed	1 oz/25g	*neg*	140
oats, regular/porridge	1 oz/25g	20	100
jumbo	1 oz/25g	20	100
oil, vegetable	1 tblsp/15mlsp	—	135
olives, stoned	1 oz/25g	—	25
onions, fresh, raw	1 lb/450g	25	100
spring, fresh, raw	1 bunch	*neg*	30
oranges, fresh	1 large	10	40
orange juice, unsweetened	¼ pint/150ml	15	60
concentrate, unsweetened	1 fl oz/25ml	20	80
parsley	1 bunch	*neg*	10
parsnips, fresh, raw, whole	1 lb/450g	40	160
passion fruit, fresh	1 lb/450g	10-12	65
pasta, wholewheat, raw	1 lb/450g	300	1490
peaches, dried	1 large	10	40
canned in natural juice	1x10 oz/284g can	30	110
fresh	1 large	10	40
peanuts, plain, shelled	1 oz/25g	*neg*	150
peanut butter, natural	1 oz/25g	5	160
pears, canned in natural juice	1x8 oz/227g can	25	100
dried	1 large	10	40
fresh	1 large	10	40
peas, fresh/frozen, cooked	1 lb/450g	20	180
peas, split, dried	1 oz/25g	15	80

Food	Amount	CHO (approx.)	Calories (approx.)
peppers, fresh, raw	4 medium	10	70
pigeon peas, dried	1 oz/25g	14	75
pineapple, canned in natural juice	1x8 oz/227g can	35	130
fresh, whole	1 lb/450g	28	110
pineapple juice, unsweetened	¼ pint/150ml	18	75
pine kernels	1 oz/25g	3	160
pistachio nuts, shelled, raw	1 oz/25g	4	150
pitta bread, wholewheat	1 average	40-50	220
plums, fresh, whole	1 lb/450g	40	160
potatoes, fresh, raw, whole	1 lb/450g	80	340
cooked	2 oz/50g	10	40
prunes, pitted	1 large	5	20
pumpkin, fresh, raw, whole	1 lb/450g	12	55
radishes, fresh	1 lb/450g	5	30
raisins	1 oz/25g	16	60
raspberries, fresh	1 lb/450g	25	120
rhubarb, fresh, raw, prepared	1 lb/450g	5	30
rice, brown, raw	1 lb/450g	350	1620
flakes, raw	1 lb/450g	360	1650
rum	1 fl oz/25ml	neg	65
satsumas, fresh	2 average	10	40
semolina, wholewheat	1 oz/25g	17	90
seeds, sesame	1 oz/25g	5	140
sunflower	1 oz/25g	5	140
sherry, dry	1 fl oz/25ml	neg	30
soy sauce	1 tblsp/15mlsp	neg	10
strawberries, fresh	1 lb/450g	25	115
sultanas	1 oz/25g	16	60
sweetcorn, canned	1x12 oz/340g can	60	280
fresh/frozen cooked	1 oz/25g	5	20
spinach, fresh, raw	1 lb/450g	15-20	100
spring greens, fresh, raw	1 lb/450g	5	20
swede, fresh, raw, whole	1 lb/450g	15	80
sweet potatoes, fresh, raw, whole	1 lb/450g	80	360
tahini (sesame paste)	1 oz/25g	5	140
tangerines, fresh	2 average	10	40
tomatoes, canned	1x14 oz/400g can	10	50
fresh, raw	1 lb/450g	10	60

Food	Amount	CHO (approx.)	Calories (approx.)
tomato juice	¼ pint/150ml	5	25
tomato purée	1 oz/25g	3	20
turnips, fresh, raw, whole	1 lb/450g	15	75
walnuts	1 oz/25g	neg	130
watercress, fresh	1 bunch	neg	20
wheatgerm	1 oz/25g	12	60
whisky	1 fl oz/25ml	neg	65
wholewheat grains	1 oz/25g	16	85
wine, red, dry	1 fl oz/25ml	neg	20
white, dry	1 fl oz/25ml	neg	20
yeast extract	1 tsp/5mlsp	neg	10
yogurt, low fat, natural	1 small pot	10	80

Manufactured Foods

(Some useful store cupboard items.)

Breakfast Cereals:			
All Bran	1 oz/25g	13	70
Shredded Wheat	1	18	80
Weetabix	1	12	60
Weetaflakes (Weetabix Ltd.)	1 oz/25g	19	95

Crispbreads:			
Krispen, Wholewheat and Bran	1	3½	15
Wholemeal Rye	1	3½	16
RyKing, Golden Wheat	1	8	38
Light	1	7	28
Brown Rye	1	8	33
Ryvita, Original	1	6	26
Brown Rye	1	6	26

Jams:			
Whole Earth, all flavours except,			
pear and apple	1 oz/25g	9	35
pear and apple	1 oz/25g	18	70

Snacks:			
Jordans Original Crunchy Bars, Coconut and Honey	1	20	155

Food	Amount	CHO (approx.)	Calories (approx.)
Honey and Almond	1	20	160
Prewetts Fruit Bars,			
Apple and Date	1	23	100
Date and Fig	1	26	110
Fruit and Bran	1	23	115
Fruit and Nut	1	23	145
Muesli Fruit	1	21	125
Banana Bar	1	18	80
Marks and Spencer Muesli			
Biscuits	1	10	80
Wholemeal Bran Biscuits	1	9	65
Sainsbury's Wholemeal Bran			
Biscuits	1	10	70

Recommended Reading

International Vegetarian Health Food Handbook (The Vegetarian Society).
Dayplan 2 (The Vegetarian Society).
J. W. Lucas, *Vegetarian Nutrition* (The Vegetarian Society).
Rodger Doyle, *The Vegetarian Handbook of Nutrition* (Thorsons Publishers Ltd.).
Countdown — A Guide to the Carbohydrate and Calorie Content of Manufactured Foods (The British Diabetic Association).

The following books have been written for Diabetics and are not vegetarian. However, much of the guidance and the vegetarian recipes (where present) are useful for anyone interested in a healthier diet which does not include meat.

J. W. Anderson MD, *Diabetes — A Practical New Guide to Healthy Living* (Martin Dunitz).
Dr Jim Mann and the Oxford Dietetic Group, *The Diabetic's Diet Book* (Martin Dunitz).
Jill Metcalfe, *Better Cookery For Diabetics* (The British Diabetic Association).

Useful Addresses

The Vegetarian Society (UK) Ltd.
Parkdale
Dunham Road
Altrincham
Cheshire

53 Marloes Road
Kensington
London W8

The British Diabetic Association
10 Queen Anne Street
London W1

The Health Education Council
78 New Oxford Street
London WC1

The British Nutrition Foundation
15 Belgrave Square
London SW1

Health Food Manufacturers Association
The Old Coach House
Southborough Road
Surbiton
Surrey

The British Dietetic Association
Daimler House
Paradise Street
Birmingham

Index